# SOURCES FOR THE HISTORY OF ENGLISH NONCONFORMITY 1660-1830

G000045257

## Michael Mullett

Senior Lecturer in History at the University of Lancaster

## British Records Association

Archives and the User                    No. 8

1991

Dedication

To Ivan Roots

ISBN : 0 900222 09 3

# CONTENTS

The cover picture, a Quarterly Circuit Plan of Northern England, 1773, appears
by kind permission of Dr John Walton of Lancaster University.

## Acknowledgements

Any historical researcher accumulates an immense debt of gratitude to those who make his materials available, and it is in the nature of this present exercise that my obligations are all the greater. I am deeply indebted to the courtesy, efficiency, expertise and helpfulness of the archivists and staff of: Dr William's Library, London, and especially Mr John Creasey for his expert guidance; the United Reformed Church Historical Society, London, and especially Mr Fred Keay; the John Rylands Library of the University of Manchester and in particular Miss Alison Peacock of the Methodist Archives; Friends House Library, London, and especially Malcolm Thomas; Mr P Grisenthwaite and the staff of the Cumbria Record Office, Kendal; the University of Lancaster Library, especially Miss T J Goodman and the staff of Inter Library Loans; and the Lancashire Record Office, Preston.

Research work on this project was made possible by a generous travel grant from the British Academy and I am especailly grateful to Miss Jane Lyddon for her help and advice. Sabbatical leave from the University of Lancaster enabled me to write up the research and my colleague in the Lancaster History department forebore with my obsession. Stuart Mews read some of my material in draft and put his vast knowledge of Methodism at my disposal. My wife Lorna helped my research and gave constant support and encouragement to the task. Alan Thacker suggested this project and, together with Aidan Lawes, who succeeded him as series editor, has provided skilled, meticulous and imaginative editorship.

Lancaster
On the Feast of the Triumph of the Cross,
1989

## Abbreviations

| | |
|---|---|
| C.R.O. | Cumbria Record Office, Kendal |
| D.W.L. | Dr Williams's Library, London |
| F.H.L | Friends House Library, London |
| J.R.L. | John Rylands Library, Manchester |
| L.R.O. | Lancashire Record Office, Preston |
| P.R.O. | Public Record Office |
| U.R.C.L. | United Reformed Church Historical Society, London |

# CHAPTER 1

# INTRODUCTION

This survey sets out to examine some of the records of the English Nonconformist and Dissenting Churches, the 'unestablished' churches, in the period from c. 1660 to 1830. It is not, of course, in any way implied that English Protestant religious dissidence did not exist before 1660 nor, certainly, that Nonconformity ceased to exist after 1828. However, the expulsions of the 'puritan' element from the re-established Church of England between 1660 and 1662 gave English Nonconformity a distinctly etched identity and a sense of social separation which survived until at least the emancipation of 1828.

The survey is arranged in a series of chapters each devoted to a denomination or a group of linked denominations. This arrangement needs to be approached with care, since it implies clear sectarian and denominational frontiers, differentiations and self-awarenesses that were not always present. In some groups and especially, as we shall see, in churches within the Presbyterian tradition, overt denominational self-recognition was weak and congregations referred to themselves simply as 'Protestant Dissenters', without any additional identification : denominational identities might also become indistinct or lost when particular bodies fused. Two groups that had their origins in Calvinistic puritanism, the Presbyterians and Independents, sometimes achieved close co-operation and even, for a period, virtual jointure, so that the nomenclature Presbyterian and Independent was, at least for a while, consigned to the category of 'formerly called'. In addition, identifying labels could lose much of their meaning when Nonconformist bodies changed their theological orientation. Some Nonconformists were able to respond freely to new currents in 18th-century English theology. In particular, English Presbyterians, and some Baptists, were especially open to non-trinitarian theological insights, so that yesterday's 'Presbyterian' congregation might become tomorrow's 'Unitarian' church, but might refer to itself as 'Protestant Dissenter', or even, still as 'Presbyterian'. For a number of reasons then, denominational titles need to be deployed with some caution, and although we shall use these labels, it will be done, in some cases, in a quite tentative way.

Experiments in Nonconformist unity have an archival interest in their own right but, clearly, cannot be fitted into the archival corpus of any one denomination. Despite bitter divisions between the two principal wings of Anglo-Calvinism, Presbyterianism and Independency during the English Revolution, in the 1650s, their pastors, especially in the North-West, collaborated closely. They brought their ministers together in many parts of the country in a 'Happy Union' between 1691 and 1695 and in the heavily Nonconformist West Country maintained such a union, based on Exeter, until 1753[1].

The Exeter Assembly was a clerical body and its orderly and systematic minutes reflect the educational attainments of its members and clerks. From its inception, following the Revolution and the Toleration Act, the Assembly was devoting some part of its recorded proceedings to the demands of an altered political situation. On the one hand, the minutes express diffidence about political involvement: 'not ... to intermeddle with State affairs'[2]; on the other hand, the Assembly's minutes are much concerned with the special interests of the joint bodies in their relations with governments, for example in soliciting an Act of Parliament 'in favour of our private Academies...'.[3]

Other matters featuring regularly in the minuted deliberations of the United Brethren included supervision of book publishing, training of ministers, precautions against frauds, contributions to building new meeting houses, the maintenance of theological orthodoxy, especially against 'Arminianism and Socinianism', the examination of ministers and their allocation to churches, the avoidance of faction and 'caballing', the disciplining of errant colleagues, and the resolution of questions, sometimes abstruse, of moral casuistry.

Unlike the United Brethren, which seemed, at least occasionally, anxious to advance to closer union, the London area's Protestant Dissenting Ministers of the Three Denominations was an alliance, not a fusion.[5] This inter-denominational committee of seven Presbyterian, six Independent and six 'Antipedobaptist' (i.e. Baptist) ministers originally met in a London coffee house and had a small budget. Its minutes are orderly, neat and legible, invariably giving a list of those present at meetings, a record of matters agreed, and regular schedules of the recognised ministers of the denominations in the London area. Earlier passages of the minutes may, however, disappoint the researcher by the meagreness of their content, being concerned, somewhat introvertedly, with the committee itself, its membership and procedures. However, in the later 18th century the minutes show the representative ministers widening their concerns, to take in the extension of the Toleration Act and the campaign against slavery.[6]

Deeply concerned with modulating the relations between the denominations from which it was recruited, the London committee showed constant vigilance lest one denomination gain an advantage over the others in terms of 'public appearances', especially at Court. Its twin brief of managing inter-denominational relations and relations between the denominations and the establishment tended to squeeze 'religious' concerns out of the ministerial committee's records, apart from the occasional rather routine condemnation of the 'decay' of 'practical religion'. The fundamental allegiance of Nonconformists to the Hanoverian Succession is evident throughout these minutes, with their regular plans for complimentary Court visits and addresses, a central purpose of which was 'to address his Majesty upon all proper Occasions in order to testify their Loyalty to his person and Government ...'.[7] A particular aspect of this basic Hanoverianism was the expression of evident relief, in 1746, at the government's 'late glorious victory over the Rebels... in Scotland'.[8]

As we have seen, the Exeter Assembly's records point to sustained attempts at integration within Nonconformity, while those of the Three Denominations bespeak harmonious co-operation along with separate development. The operations of these area bodies have left us archival sources which are characterised by order, clarity, accuracy and method (even so, the 'secretary and scribes' of the

Three Denominations were rebuked on one occasion for missing out an important item of business).[9] These groups of records form indispensable sources for the study of collaboration or unification in 17th- and 18th-century Nonconformity, the joint work of regional clergy and the steady evolution of committee procedures.

In this survey of Nonconformist records, we shall be heavily concerned with collective church records, and in particular with sources which are, in effect, minute books. We must also consider some more individually oriented sources which throw light on the life of the Nonconformist churches in our period. High on any list of these are letters, such as the vast manuscript correspondence at Dr. Williams's Library of one of the 17th century's most noteworthy 'Reformed' pastors, Richard Baxter (1615-1691).[10]

A useful source for the history of Nonconformity, especially in the early years after 1662, is autobiography, especially of Nonconformist ministers. Again, Richard Baxter provides an excellent example. His *Autobiography*[11] brings together characteristic introspection with reflections on the genesis of formal Nonconformity and on wider public matters, especially as far as they concerned Nonconformists. The *Autobiography, Diaries, Anecdotes and Event Books* of the ejected Yorkshire minister, Oliver Heywood (1630-1702)[12], combine personal notes with sharply pointed observations on the misfortunes of public sinners such as Sabbath-breakers. The autobiography of another northern ejected minister, Adam Martindale (1623-1686)[13], includes vivid recollections on the fate of the dispossessed ministers of 1662. One of these, Thomas Jolly (1629-1703)[14] recalled some of his post-Restoration experiences in particularly graphic terms, though characteristic of the genre:

> Upon the 17th of August, 1662, Captain Bannister, Captain Nowell, and Ensign Grimshaw, brought a suspension, ... and forced me out of the public place, .. I withdrew, leaving this admonition with Captain Bannister, that this was not the way to turn away the wrath of God from his house, which had long been upon it ... . Thus was I thrust out of the place where I had laboured for nigh thirteen years, ... . Upon my seclusion from Altham I broke up house; myself and three young children put to wander for a considerable time without any certain dwelling place.. . [Subsequently] the Lord, in a most dreadful manner, took off one of them by death, viz. Mr John Grimshaw ... . He died in the prosecution of his most debauched practices and with inexpressible horror.[15]

Some Nonconformist autobiographies are, of course, spiritual classics in their own right: above all John Bunyan's *Grace Abounding to the Chief of Sinners*.[16] Not, perhaps, a spiritual classic, the *Autobiography of William Stout of Lancaster 1665-1752*[17] takes us deep into the ordinary, daily life of provincial Dissent. A long-serving clerk of various Lancashire Quaker meetings, Stout was a small-scale local businessman displaying economic and moral attitudes which some historians think typical of the Georgian Nonconformist bourgeois laity. Stout's deep-dyed Whiggery on the political front can certainly be taken as representative of his species. Less morally intact than Stout, the diary of the south Lancashire Presbyterian-inclined Roger Lowe reveals a theologically literate layman trying to square puritan convictions with the routine self-indulgences of popular culture.[18] Apart from these one-man clerical and lay autobiographies, early Nonconformity came to acquire a kind of collective clerical biography, or hagiography, notably in Edmund Calamy's *The Nonconformist's Memorial: Being an Account of the Ministers, who were Ejected or Silenced after the Restoration particularly by the Act of Uniformity*.[19]

The range of commentary and official record set down by conformists about Nonconformists forms an important 'external' source. A high proportion of this material comes from the immediate post-Restoration period when the existence of Protestant religious dissidence was a major political issue. Provincial sources such as the Corie Letters[20] give us a picture of the establishment and strength of Nonconformity in England's second city, and of the alarm it caused in official quarters, especially fears of 'Anabaptist' dissidence in the troubled 1660s. In his own world, of Kendal and rural Westmorland, justice Daniel Fleming was a zealous repressor of Protestant recusancy.[21] Especially in the years after 1660, Anglicans tried to gauge the numerical state of non-Anglican Protestantism. These recurrent efforts tended to represent not any dispassionate quest for statistics as such but rather attempts either to raise the alarm about an alleged numerical danger to the Church or to show that a battle was being won and that the strength of Dissent was being eroded. The most important, if incomplete, survey was the so-called 'Compton census' of 1676, commissioned under the strongly Anglican ministry of Lord Treasurer Danby. The superb recent edition of this source by Dr Anne Whiteman[22] is itself a major event in archival work.

An important external and official source for the history of Nonconformity is the long series of registrations and licences for non-Anglican Protestants to congregate and worship following Charles II's abortive Declaration of Indulgence of 1672. Names of individuals and premises were recorded for permitted worship, until the arguably unconstitutional royal Declaration was hastily withdrawn, under parliamentary and episcopal pressure, in 1673. The licences of this brief period of indulgence are in Lambeth Palace Library and the Public Record Office and the subject can be studied in material edited by G. Lyon Turner.[23] A 1672 licence may yield considerable information to the student of the history of Nonconformity: for instance, that the royal Declaration met a ready and positive response from many Nonconformists; that the building of meeting houses proceeded to some extent after the publication of the Declaration on 16 March; and that the law-abiding Presbyterians, unlike the more uncompromising Quakers in the 1670s, built, or otherwise set up, meeting houses only when they had some colour of legal clearance to do so. The following is an example of a 1672 licence:

> License to John Harvie to be a Pr. [Presbyterian] Teacher in a meeting-house in Tockley [Tockholes] erected for that purpose in the Parish of Blackburn, Lancaster. [Lancs.] 1 May '72.
> The meeting house in Tockley in the parish of Blackburn in Lancashire Pr. Meeting, 8 May '72.

However, this Lancashire meeting house, specially built for the purpose, is not typical of the Nonconformists nationally: in Wiltshire, the 70 licences taken out by the Presbyterians (46 of the whole), Independents and Baptists were all for existing houses or barns.[24]

Although the 1672 'Indulgence', like its successors under James II, failed to achieve any permanent standing, parliamentary toleration enshrined in the Toleration Act of 1689 allowed nonconforming congregations to meet (behind unlocked doors), subject to the requirement that 'the place of such meeting shall be certified to the bishop of the diocese, or to the archdeacon of the archdeaconry, or to the justices of the peace at the general or quarter sessions of the peace .. and registered ... or recorded...; the register or clerk of the peace ... to give certificate thereof to such persons as shall demand the same ...'. Thus under this system, which remained in place until 1812 and in an altered form thereafter until 1852, the diocesan or county authorities recorded registrations and the congregations received certificates. Since these certificates were the visible expression of the Toleration Act's protective terms, congregations did indeed 'demand the same'.[25]

Dr. Peskett is right to criticise some of the short-comings of the certificates in terms of the information that they provide, in particular their 'imprecision as to denomination'.[26] Thus a typical early certificate gives us a certain amount of information, but not the denomination in question, least of all when it is Presbyterian in orientation :

> 1710 - Certificate of Justices in Session, for Services in Tockholes Chapel - Lancc. SS::
> These are to certifye that a Generall Qr. Sessions of the Peace be held by adjournment at Wiggan, in and for the County Pallatine of Lancaster, the Nynth day of October; Anno Dni. One thousand Seaven hundred and Tenn, A certaine Ediffice, newly erected within Livesey-in-Tockholes in the said County is recorded for a Meeting-place for an Assembly of persons dissenting ffrom the Church of England, for the exercise of their religious worshipp, pursuant to an Act of Parliament entituled An Act for Exempting their Majesties' Protestant Subjects dissenting from the Church of England from the Pennaltyes of certaine Lawes, ....[27]

The final phrases of that certificate partly explains why the looked-for denominational tag is missing: the statute conferred its benefits on an undifferentiated (though selected) mass of 'Protestant subjects dissenting from the Church of England', and the law took no account of doctrinal and ecclesiological demarcations apart from the basic fact of dissent from the Church. To some extent, such deficiencies of vital classifying information can be made good from some of the applications for certificates where these are available, as in the case of a 1696 plea for certification and registration of 'a Meeting House newly erected for the worshipp of Almighty God by his Majesty's loyal Protestant subjects, the Dissenters of Bolton and the adjacent parts, commonly called Presbyterians'.[28] In addition, denominational information seems to have been included in the certificates themselves on a more regular, but not invariable, basis (if the Wiltshire case is anything to go by) from about the 1730s onwards.[29]

Information provided in the meeting house certificates is, of course, indispensable to the historian of Nonconformity for building up any complete picture of its development, especially on the statistical front. However, Nonconformists were themselves anxious to obtain as complete a statistical picture as possible of individual bodies and of Nonconformity as a whole. The late-seventeenth century age of Gregory King fell in love with data, and something of this enthusiasm can be seen in an ambitious plan of the Exeter-based Devon and Cornwall Assemblies for a Nonconformist central registry in London, 'to receive all the accounts that shall be given in from time to time that they may digest them methodically; which Register shall contain a general idea of the whole Nonconformist interest in the Kingdom'.[30]

Such a scheme was prompted by more than just statistical curiosity: the numerical prosperity or otherwise of Nonconformity might carry important messages of religious encouragement or dejection, while in the continuing negotiations between Nonconformity and the state it was important to have an idea of what the size of the Nonconformist 'interest' was. A Presbyterian statistical report of 1690-2[31] was part of an attempt to deploy the strength of Nonconformity to best effect. The most important piece of internal Nonconformist demography was the survey, denomination by denomination, carried out by the committee of the Three Denominations between 1715 and 1718.[32] Recordings of the survey were made by the Presbyterian minister John Evans and by the Independent, Daniel Neal. Neal's list was subsequently incorporated in a further survey by the Baptist, Josiah Thompson, in 1772-3.[33]

As we shall see in the course of this study, the Nonconformists kept human statistics of varying degrees of exhaustiveness: lists of members and of births/ baptisms, marriages and deaths. The Baptists, predictably enough, kept full baptismal registers. In general terms, the Nonconformist churches in our period can be roughly divided between those with comparatively open relations with the world outside and those with more sectarian identities. The latter groups tended to have more definite data on membership, more stringent discipline so as to differentiate members' standards from those of surrounding society, and more absolute demands on their members' loyalties. The Society of Friends provides an example. In addition, the Quakers' persistent adherence to their own marriages and funerals secured for them unusual privileges in holding, and consequently recording, these events. The Quaker founder, George Fox (1624-1691), ordered the keeping of registers in 1656 and many Quaker register series begin in the late 1660s. In 1776 a new system of form-filling was introduced. The overall result was, as Dr. Peskett says, that '... Quaker registers are outstanding, far superior to any other Nonconformist Church'.[34]

In general, and certainly from Hardwicke's Marriage Act of 1753, the only non-Anglican Protestant marriages valid in England and Wales were those of the Friends, so non-Quaker Nonconformist marriage registers are not a serious category in our period. Recorded funeral services and burials are, as we shall see, another matter, and baptisms were purely voluntary ceremonies which might be, and were, freely recorded. Whether, as with the Quakers, the demographic record was complete, or whether, as with other denominations, it was patchy, between 1837 and 1858 the state, with considerable success as far as the Nonconformists were concerned, sought to call in all registers to the office of the Registrar General, offering in return legally valid copies. The original Nonconformist registers thereby became public records and are now in the Public Record Office.[35]

Far from being accepted as public records, some denominational archives were occasionally regarded as private property. Thus we hear stories like that of a late-18th century Baptist deacon who died in possession of church records which his family simply refused to return, the archive eventually being destroyed as lumber. Archives have also been victims of pique and schism: when in 1749 Howell Harris withdrew from the English Calvinistic Methodist Association, he took with him to Trevecka the minutes of the London Tabernacle so that 'those minutes simply came to an end'.[36]

In a survey of the limited length of this one, much must be omitted. Though for much of the time we shall be citing examples from manuscript sources, it is important to realise how many church records have appeared in print: Dr Watts provides a list.[37] For the manuscript sources, apart from the excellent surveys by Peskett, Steel and Welch, referred to above, there is a comprehensive list of materials held in Dr. Williams's Library.[38] The more one sees of such Nonconformist records, the more one is struck by their stylistic heterogeneity. On the whole, the individual congregations kept what records they liked, dealing with matters they considered important. There was often little in the way of a central organisation to dictate the kind of stereotyping of form that we find, for example, in many of the proceedings of the Church of England. We shall not be able to say, for example, 'the following is a standard example of the recorded disciplinary procedures of the Independents'. Therefore, for much of the time in this survey we shall be sampling and tasting, in the process encountering a wide range of forms, styles and content.

It is important in any archival study not to tamper overmuch with the written form of the originals. Abbreviations from originals will be retained, sometimes with explanatory amplificatiions in square brackets. However, 'the' and 'that' will appear in full and the 17th-and 18th century custom of raising abbreviated letters above the line of manuscript will be dispensed with.

Most of the sources we shall be encountering in this survey are record books of church meetings and registers of the births, marriages and deaths of members. The registration books are self-explanatory, but a word or two needs to be said about books of minutes. Worship sessions were, of course, seldom recorded except for special occasions such as ordinations to the ministry. We shall be examining  the records of church meetings chiefly for business, covering the matters in which the administration of these churches was concerned. Business meetings, perhaps of select members, perhaps of the whole membership of a gathered church, came together periodically, typically on a monthly basis. There were important differences in the emphasis that different churches within Nonconformity gave to different matters: in particular, the more sectarianised bodies such as the Baptists and Quakers gave more attention to moral discipline that did those with a more open and 'denominational' relationship to the outside world such as the Presbyterians. The proceedings of these periodic sessions for business were entered up by clerks who served on a voluntary basis, though sometimes there were honoraria for this kind of work. There were few if any standard procedures either between churches or within churches, though the Quakers and the Methodists, with their national bodies, had more stylistic and secretarial uniformity than other bodies. A common format was for the proceedings of meetings to be entered in a fairly imposing and substantial volume known by such a title as 'church book'. Minutes of business meetings of local congregations, especially the smaller ones, might be entered, two, three or more to the page, while great sessions, like Methodist national conferences, would run over several pages.

Finally in this introductory chapter, the student will want to know something of the location of English Dissenter archives and of material pertaining to Dissenters. I shall sub-divide the treatment of location of material into the main categories of national public archives, county record offices and national Nonconformist collections.[39]

*National collections*

The Hunter mss. in the British Library include (Add. Ms. 24884) a survey of post-Restoration Independent and Presbyterian congregations. The Public Record Office has extensive resources for compiling a social and demographic history of Dissenters, including such material as a listing of Quakers affirming (rather than swearing oaths) so as to qualify as attorneys. From 1736, trust deeds belonging to congregations were entered on the Close Rolls (P.R.O. , C 54). The P.R.O. also holds (RG 4, RG 6 and RG 8) around 9,000 Nonconformist registers of births, marriages and deaths submitted to the Registrar General under mid-19th century legislation; other items, including minutes, and diaries of the minister, were often inserted into these deposited registers. At St Catherine's House, Kingsway, London, are materials on chapel registration, entered under the new system following the cessation of the Toleration Act's arrangements for certification in 1852, documentation making it possible to establish the foundation dates of then extant Nonconformist congregations. Over 54,000 of these registrations (including Roman Catholic, from 1791) were in fact submitted to the Registrar General, but though the submissions have the advantage for the historian of concentrating material in a central location, local quarter sessions clerks and Church registrars varied considerably in the thoroughness of their compliance with the Registrar General's requirements. Even so, the overall result for the historian of the replacement of the old certification system and of the Victorian insistence on good statistics and its legislative outcome, has been to provide a remarkable central corpus of material giving a retrospective view, from a mid-19th century vantage point, back to the origins of Nonconformity, its members and its congregations.[40] As we have seen, considerable material illuminating Nonconformist history, especially the various post-Restoration surveys, can be found in the archives of the Church of England.

## County Record Offices

There has been a trend, positively encouraged by some denominations, to lodge historical material belonging to Nonconformist communities in the counties in their county record offices, where security, public access and care of documents can be guaranteed. Apart from minute books, financial documents, registers, collections of letters etc. produced by Dissenting congregation in counties and eventually deposited in county record offices,[41] these offices may also contain material of a public and legal nature having a bearing upon Nonconformists. Examples of this latter category are the subscriptions, required under the Toleration Act, of Dissenters to the bulk of the Thirty-Nine Articles, and also copies of returns made under the Act of 1829 which required lists, township by township, of 'the number of places of worship, not of the Church of England, ... of what sect or persuasion, ...' .[42] Two major classes of county record office legal records are, obviously, of immense importance for the history of Dissent. These are the regular presentments of Nonconformists, from the reign of Elizabeth to 1689, for non-attendance at church, presentments entered in quarter sessions rolls or in justices' note-books and, after 1689, there are meeting house certifications, generally entered in quarter sessions order books and in bishops' and archdeacons' registers'.[43]

## Nonconformist national collections

These are located in the capital or in other centres. Dr Williams's Library, 14 Gordon Square, London, is a kind of national archives and library for Dissent[44] with the Evans, Lyon Turner, Thompson and Wilson manuscripts and Presbyterian/Unitarian records (including the minutes of the Presbyterian Fund), as well as Baptist material (some on microfilm). The nearby archives of the United Reformed Church, 86 Tavistock Place, London has Presbyterian material, along with a store of church histories, especially from London and the North. As we have seen, Baptist material is available in Dr Williams's Library; also at Regent's Park College, Pusey Street, Oxford and in the hands of local churches. Sources for Independent congregations are also often in local churches and local record offices, with some archives, especially those of London congregations, being kept at the Memorial Hall, Fleet Lane, London. The great Methodist Archives and Research Collection at the John Rylands Library, Deansgate, Manchester, includes Wesleyana, circuit plans, minutes of administrative bodies at all levels of Methodism, and material from most of Methodism's historical variants. Justly celebrated, the Library of the Society of Friends, Friends' House, Euston Road, London, functions as both an archive for the national and metropolitan meetings of the Quakers and also as a guide to Quaker research sources nationwide.

### Notes to Chapter 1

1. *The Exeter Assembly. The Minutes of the Assemblies of the United Brethren of Devon and Cornwall, 1691-1717,* ed. Allen Brockett and others, Devon and Cornwall Record Soc., new ser., vi (1963), intro., p. vii ff. For the records of other bodies engendered by Presbyterian-Independent unification, see below Ch. V.

2. *Ibid.,* p. 1.

3. *Ibid.,* p. 26.

4. *Ibid.,* pp. 5, 6, 17, 21-2, 25, 28, 35-6, 41-3.

5. D.W.L.: Minute Book of the Body of Protestant Dissenting Ministers of the Three Denominations in and about the Cities of London and Westminster, 3 vols.

6. *Ibid.,* vol. II, p. 195, ff., 261.

7. *Ibid.,* p. 40 (1763).

8. *Ibid.,* vol. I, p. 129, 134.

9. *Ibid.,* p. 49.

10. A selection of Quaker epistolary sources is available in A. R. Barclay, ed., *Letters of Early Friends* (London, 1841); for John Wesley see J. Telford's edition of his *Letters* (8 vols., London, 1931).

11. Richard Baxter, *Autobiography: being the Reliquiae Baxterianae,* ed. J. J. Lloyd Thomas (London, 1931).

12. Ed. J. Horsfall Turner (4 vols., Brighouse and Bingley, Yorks., 1882-5).

13. *Life of Adam Martindale,* ed. R. Parkinson, Chetham Soc., iv (1845).

14. *Note Book of the Rev. Thomas Jolly, A.D. 1671-1693....,* ed. Henry Fishwick, Chetham Soc., new ser., xxxiii (1894).

15. Quoted in Abel Jones Parry, *History of the Cloughold Baptist Church, From 1675 to 1875* (Manchester, n.d.), pp. 33-4.

16.    A good edition by Roger Sharrock, (Oxford, 1962).

17.    Ed. J. D. Marshall, Manchester: Chetham Soc., 1967.

18.    *The Diary of R. Lowe ...*, ed. W. L. Sachse (London, 1938).

19.    Various editions: e.g. by Samuel Palmer (2 vols., London, 1775). See also the supplement to Calamy, A. G. Matthews, *Calamy Revised: Being a Revision of Edmund Calamy's Account ...* (Oxford, 1934, reissued 1988).

20.    Ed. R. Hill, Norfolk Record Soc., xxvii, 1956.

21.    See Historical Manuscripts Commission, *Manuscripts of S. H. Le Fleming, Esq. ...* (London, 1890).

22.    *The Compton Census of 1676. A Critical Edition* (Records of Social and Economic History, new ser., x, London, 1986). See also: Anne Whiteman, 'The Census that Never Was', in Anne Whiteman and others, *Statesmen, Scholars and Merchants: Essays in Eighteenth-Century History Presented to Dame Lucy Sutherland* (Oxford, 1973), pp. 1-16; T. Richards, 'The Religious Census of 1676', *Trans. Hon. Soc of Cymmrodorion* (1925-6), supplement; S.A.Peyton, 'The Religious Census of 1676', *English Historical Review*, xlviii (1933), pp. 9-104.

23.    In *Original Records of Early Nonconformity under Persecution and Indulgence* (3 vols., London, 1911-1914); see also the valuable study by Frank Bate, *The Declaration of Indulgence 1672: A Study in the Rise of Organised Dissent* (London, 1908).

24.    B. Nightingale, *History of the Old Independent Chapel, Tockholes, Near Blackburn, Lancashire ...* (London and Manchester, 1886), p. 33; *Wiltshire Dissenters' Meeting House Certificates and Registrations, 1689-1852*, ed. J. H. Chandler, Wiltshire Record Soc., xl (1985), Appendix.

25.    See also: E. Welch, 'The Registration of Meeting Houses', *Journal Soc. Archivists*, iii (1966), pp. 116-120; for regional examples: J. Varley, 'Dissenters' Certificates in the Lincoln Diocesan Record', *Lincolnshire Historian*, iv (1949); Barbara Donaldson, 'Registration of Dissenting Chapels', *Staffordshire Record Soc.*, 4th ser., iii (1960); and Chandler, ed., *Wiltshire Certificates, passim* ·

26.    Hugh Peskett, 'Guide to the Parish and Non-Parochial
       Registers of Devon and Cornwall 1538-1837', *Devon and
       Cornwall Record Soc.*, extra ser., ii (1979), p. xlviii.

27.    Nightingale, *History of the Old Independent Chapel,
       Tockholes*, pp. 37-8.

28.    [Anon], *Bank Street Chapel, Bolton. Bi-Centenary
       Commemoration, 1696-1896*, (London and Manchester,
       n.d.), p. 31.

29.    Chandler, ed., *Wiltshire Certificates, passim*.

30.    Brockett, ed., *Exeter Assmbly*, p. 19.

31.    Peskett, 'Guide to the Registers', p. xlvi.

32.    D. W. L.: MS. 38, 4. For a full consideration of the
       survey, see Michael Watts, *The Dissenters. From
       the Reformation to the French Revolution* (Oxford,
       1978), Appendix, pp. 491-508.

33.    D. W. L.: MS. 38, 5.

34.    Peskett, 'Guide to the Registers', p. lxi.

35.    See: D. J. Steel, *National Index of Parish Registers,
       vol. II: Sources for Nonconformist Genealogy and Family
       History* (Chichester, 1973-4); Edwin Welch,
       'Nonconformist Registers', *Journal Soc. Archivists*,
       ii (1964), pp. 235-8 (with addresses of archives);
       L. W. Lawson Edwards, *Index to Cornish Nonconformist
       Registers Deposited at the Public Record Office*
       (London, 1976).

36.    Jones Parry, *History of Cloughold Baptist Church*,
       p. 47; *Two Calvinistic Methodist Chapels 1743-1811.
       The London Tabernacle and Spa Fields Chapel*,
       ed. Edwin Welch, London Record Soc., xi (1975), p. xi.

37.    In *The Dissenters*, p. 512.

38.    *Nonconformist Congregations in Great Britain: a list
       of histories and other material in Dr Williams's
       Library* (1973). See also: British Records Association,
       *The Archives of Ecclesiastical Bodies other than the
       Church of England* (Report from Committees, no. 3,
       1936); and W. R. Powell and others, 'Protestant
       Nonconformist Records', *Archives*, v (1961), pp. 1-12.

39.    See also: W. B. Stephens, *Sources for English Local History*
       (2nd ed., Cambridge, 1981), pp. 268-286; F. G. Emmison,
       *Archives and Local History* (London, 1966), pp. 49-50 and
       W. R. Powell, 'Bibliographical Aids to Research XII. --
       The Sources for the History of Protestant Nonconformist
       Churches in England', *Bulletin of the Institute of Historical
       Research*, xxv (1952), pp. 213-227. A most useful guide to
       research materials in the journals of learned societies is by
       E.L.C. Mullins, *A Guide to the Historical and Archaeological
       Publications of Societies in England and Wales, 1901-1933*
       (London, 1968); see its excellent index, under 'Nonconformist',
       'Nonconformity' and under particular denominations.
       There are also, by the same author, two guides to record office
       calendars - *Texts and Calendars. An Analytical Guide to Serials
       Publications*  (London,1958; reprinted with corrections, 1978)
       and *Texts and Calendars II* , (London, 1983). *Papers of British
       Churchmen 1780-1940* is No. 6 in the Royal Commission on
       Historical Manuscripts series of Guides to Sourcesfor British
       History (London, 1987) and includes information on the
       whereabouts of the papers of Nonconformist ministers.For
       research material held in individual churches, see
       Janet Smith, 'The Local Records of Nonconformity',
       *The Local Historian*, viii (1968), pp. 133-4.

40.    R. B. Rose, 'Some National Sources for Protestant
       Nonconformist and Roman Catholic History', *Bulletin
       of the Institute of Historical Research*, xxxi (1958),
       pp. 79-83.

41.    See, for example, R. Sharpe France, *Guide to the
       Lancashire Record Office* (Preston, 1985), pp. 135-148.

42.    *Ibid.*, p. 17. For an outstanding example of Nonconformist
       history on the county level and the study of its research base,
       see J. H. Hodson's'Supplement to the Introduction' of *Quarter
       Sessions Records,Trinity, 1682, to Epiphany, 1690*, ed.
       H. C. Johnson, Warwick County Records, viii (1953),
       pp. lxix-cxxxix.

43.    For addresses of County Record Offices (with those of
       some other archives discussed in this introduction), with
       their opening hours, dates and facilities, see The Royal
       Commission on Historical Manuscripts, *Record Repositories
       in Great Britain*, 8th edn., 1987).
       For addresses of libraries holding Nonconformist material
       (addresses given for the Baptists and the Methodists are
       now out of date), see C.E.Welch, 'Archives and Manuscripts
       in Nonconformist Libraries' *Archives*, vi (1963-4), pp. 236-8.

See also the excellent guide to literature on Nonconformist (plus Church of England and Catholic) archives, in Morris Garratt's 'Select Bibliography', in Garratt, ed., *Sure Coffers. Some sources for the history of religion in the North*, (Knowsley, 1987), pp. 40-8.

44.  See Kenneth Twinn, 'Sources for Church History in Dr Williams's Library' *The Local Historian*, ix (1970-1), pp. 115-120.

# CHAPTER II

# RECORDS OF THE BAPTIST CHURCH

This chapter will observe the conventional distinction between the General and Particular Baptists but will not explore a smaller sub-division, the Seventh-Day Baptists.

## The General Baptists

### Introduction
It may be possible to trace the remoter origins of the General Baptist churches to later medieval Lollard heresy, especially since the Baptists were to be found in our period in considerable numbers in such areas as Buckinghamshire, Kent and Lincolnshire where pre-Reformation Lollardy was once entrenched. Whatever we speculate, though, about distant Lollard origins of General Baptist churchmanship, its more definitely traceable roots can be identified in the early 17th century from the radical separatism and anti-predestinarian principles of John Smyth (?1570-1612) and Thomas Helwys (1550?-1616?), the latter of whom led a General Baptist church founded at Spitalfields in London in 1612. The radicalism of General Baptist ideas, including their rejection of conventional doctrines of predestination and their espousal of toleration, exposed them to considerable persecution, though their numbers, about 150 in various part of southern Engand in 1626, were not large. However, the General Baptists expanded considerably during the overall growth of religious radicalism in the 1640s and 1650s, partly through the efforts of their missionary, Henry Denne (d. 1660?), so that by 1660 they had about 110 congregations.

At the Restoration, the General Baptists' reputation for religious, social and political radicalism led once again to fierce persecution, but by 1718 they had a total of perhaps 122 congregations in England and Wales, found largely in eastern counties of England and, like all Dissenting groups, were somewhat urbanised. From 1654 onwards they held a general assembly. This body was not able to head off a major theological controversy, associated with Matthew Caffyn from the 1670s onwards, over the divinity or humanity of Christ. This issue split the General Baptists into two sub-divisions until the general acceptance of scriptural reconciling formulae, the 'six principles', in 1731. However, a degree of christological unison did not prevent subsequent trinitarian/unitarian debates and in the course of the 18th century the General Baptists were noticeably affected by the rise of unitarian theology. On the other hand, the Baptists were also touched by the Evangelical Revival, an influence seen in the New Connexion of General Baptists in 1770. This body issued minutes of general assemblies in, for example, 1787, 1795, 1802 and onwards.[1]

### Federal bodies
Like a number of other Nonconformist bodies, notably the Friends and the Methodists, the General Baptists evolved federal assemblies on both the regional and the national levels, as well as a central General Baptist Fund, with extant accounts.

23

The General Baptist General Assembly began meeting in 1654 - and subsequent christological discords produced in fact two general assemblies between 1697 and 1731, or rather a General Assembly and a rival 'Association', with its own ample minutes. Meeting annually, usually at a meeting house in London, the General Assembly possessed a degree of authority, loose or tight, supervisory or advisory, that was itself a topic of discourse in General Baptist churches. The annual Assembly was presided over by a chairman and two 'moderators', and had a battery of scribes to take the minutes. Committees were set up for special tasks. The minute book was the responsibility of a senior officer of the church. Complete runs begin in 1689 and from some point in the 18th century proceedings were printed for distribution. A typical set of minutes begins with an identifying overture:

> The Names of the Messengers Elders & Representatives of the Severall Churches of Baptized Congregations who Own the Doctrine of Universall Redemption through our Lord Jesus Christ ... Held in Glass House Yeard ... London ... 19th ... May 1725.

Names of members, messengers, elders and other representatives, in the earlier 18th century perhaps around thirty, were entered, minutes of the previous assembly were read, and correspondence arising was considered. Business might include: the affairs of particular churches, especially their ministry; individual cases of conscience and discipline from the localities; queries from local churches, for example about 'Mixt Marriages' or the permissibility of the Lord's Prayer in services; ordaining a fast day to be observed by the churches; the mission field, especially in Ireland and Virginia; prayers 'for the Safety of the Kings person now at Hanover for a blessing on his good designs ... for Defeating this present Spanish Invasion ...' (1721); and the composition of circular letters, for example, on 'the great Decay of Religion & the generall want there is of a Ministeriall help in many Churches ...'. An organisationally integrated church, the General Baptists, both on the national, and on the regional level, bear some comparison in the administrative field with another pyramidically structured body, the Society of Friends.

Individual General Baptist churches were also brought together in local associations such as those that met at various times in Buckinghamshire, Essex, Leicestershire, Lincolnshire, Northamptonshire, and Staffordshire, or in groups of counties or in a part of a county. A brief look at the minutes of one of these area bodies will give some idea of their competence and interests.

This local syndicate met from 1717 in various towns in east Kent and its orderly minutes recorded a vast range of primarily administrative transactions: finance; exchange of preachers and provision of supply preachers; arbitration between individual churches; correspondence with the churches in west Kent; inspection of individual churches and their 'Defects'; encouraging contacts between young and more experienced church members; prodding deacons into assisting the poor; keeping an area register of vital statistics; advertising job vacancies - 'openings'- for church members throughout the area; recommending book purchases and distributing copies amongst the congregations; and the setting up of a system of family visits much like that of the Society of Friends.

As part of its policy of keeping individual churches and their members up to a set mark, the area association issued sets of 'Six Questions' which bear some resemblance, at least in conception, to the Quakers' standard 'Queries' . The questionnaire concerned brotherly love in congregations; the discipline of errant individuals; the training of youth and recruitment to the ministry; the numerical state of the churches; and attention to preaching and poor relief. The routine answers to these routine queries may disappoint the researcher looking for an accurate view of the state of the Baptist churches in the regions at the time of the survey: 'The State of the Churches was enquired into and there was not anything Particular to be Noticed', or 'the state of our Churches: we are about the Same situation as before'.

### The Records of General Baptist congregations.

Below the national and regional fora, the key unit of General Baptist churchmanship was the individual local congregation. In our review of the records of these congregations, the following topics will be considered: (a) preambles and confessions of faith; (b) church discipline, in its various sub-headings; (c) the doctrine of the church; (d) church membership; (e) ministry; (f) finance; and (g) charity.

### Preambles and confessions of faith

We can expect to find in written church covenants and the preambles of minute books, if nowhere else, varying amounts of information about the distinctive tenets of Nonconformist churches. This is certainly true of the General Baptists, and it is worth looking at their church minute book preambles for the evidence these contain of theological standpoint and also of doctrinal tension. Two matters stand out in these documents: rejection of predestination, and the doctrine of Christ. The repudiation of predestination was central since the *raison d'être* of the General Baptists was an 'Arminian' confidence in general redemption. Thus a typical church minute book preamble forms a theological manifesto setting out the anti-predestinarian principles that the General Baptists had made their own:

> ...wee doe stedfastly beleeve that the unspeakable Love of ... god was Manifestly set forth And published to all the Sons And daughters of Adam In his promise to the Womans seede to break the Serpents head And was further Manifested to all Adams posterity when In the fullness of time he Made good that promis In sending forth his only begotten Son to be a Sacrifice for the Whole World. ... he is Noe Respecter of Persons: And ... hath Noe pleasure in the death of Any siner ...

It will be noticed that there is a definite, and entirely characteristic, attempt here to root this doctrine in Scripture, the Baptists' emblem. There was indeed an evident tendency to refer all questions to Scripture rather than to merely speculative theology, and to preface services with readings from Scripture. To repair rifts caused by William Caffyn's adoption of heterodox christology, in

1731 most of the General Baptist churches agreed on a common denominator of six basic scriptural principles derived from Hebrews 6: 1-2 and used as a warrant for not raising abstruse theoretical issues but concentrating instead on moral progress.

In fact, even before 1731 the 'six principles' set out in Hebrews 6: 1-2 were being inserted into the preambles to the records of individual churches and associated groups of General Baptist churches. Examples are taken from Kent, an area where Caffyn's influence had been strong:

> The Congregation of Baptized Belivers owning the six Principles of Dockt. of Christ Mentioned Ebrews. 6.1.2 Meeting in & aboute Burnham ...
> We the Meeting of the Churches of our Lord Jesus Christ in & about East Kent (Professing the principles of the Doctrine of Christ mentioned Hebrew the 6th 1:2 & the Doctrine of General Redemption) ...

Thus two marked features of General Baptists' church records, and also of area assembly records, are prefaces containing doctrinal formulations. While, as we shall see, such doctrinal statements are also to be found in the church records of other Nonconformist groups, two marked features in General Baptist preambles are an insistence on anti-predestinarian identification marks, and also forms of words which play down excessive and divisive theological precision in favour of scriptural fundamentals.

### Church discipline

Their practice of believers' baptism would point to an identification of Baptist churches as selective rather than inclusive with regard to their own membership. Such 'gathered' churches tended to be characterised by an exigent moral discipline, reflected in the sheer volume of the records of the General Baptist churches devoted to disciplinary matters. Generally speaking, this disciplinary record concerns questions of behaviour rather than doctrine. The procedure was for disciplinary cases to be dealt with in church meetings, each stage being recorded by the clerk until completion. The basic steps included admonition, then suspension from communion (pending repentance) if warnings went unheeded and the final step of expulsion with or without the possibility of later re-admission.

The profusion of General Baptist disciplinary cases will be broken down for analysis into a number of main areas: (1) disobedience to the church; (2) drink and drink-related offences; (3) sexual and marital irregularities; (4) other offences. Some idea of the overall range of General Baptist disciplinary concerns - almost certainly the largest single topic in the records of these churches - is given in a list of offences handled by one church, Dover General Baptists. As with other Nonconformist churches, the disciplinary category 'for Drunkenes' looms large, followed by 'ffor ffornication' and the 'sinn of Uncleanes & other disorders', along with 'for contention in [a] familly'. A separate procedure, rather self-defeating, dealt with 'neglect of duty & refuseing to heare admonition'. In similar fashion, the Canterbury General Baptist church included offences such as 'for marrying one out of fellowship' (compare the Quaker ban on 'marrying out') and 'unchristian behaviour', but also, again, the fundamental disciplinary offence of refusing to accept discipline. We shall deal with this as our first substantive category of General Baptist disciplinary infractions as they appear in the documents. We shall see that the way recording clerks recorded and presented repudiations of church authority contains considerable interest and some complexity.

### (1) Disobedience to the church

Challenges to the church's authority on a fairly low level of confrontation were frequently recorded when members simply absented themselves - just once or for months or years. A much more direct challenge than passive absenteeism was apostacy, especially to 'the false worship of the nation'. Some of the most spectacular instances of defiance of church authority appearing in the records of disciplinary cases arose when an individual was brought under the scrutiny of the church's, purely voluntary, disciplinary competence only to reject it:

> ...becaus he being sent unto ['for abuseing his wife'] did slight the church and in his writting question the authority of the church and allso the writting of the Apostell paulle

### (2) Drink and drink-related offences

As much as, if not more than, the records of other Nonconformist churches, the disciplinary records of the General Baptists give considerable space to the problems of excessive drinking and other associated irregularities. The Baptists, at least in the 17th and 18th centuries, were no more teetotal than their contemporaries: one congregation on one occasion authorised its deacons 'to be security to the Brewers ... on behalf of sistr ffranklin, for due paymt for such Beere as she take of them ...' Thus the disciplinary record is concerned not with drinking *per se* but with 'frequent drunknnes', which might block a member's subsequent re-admission to the church. In addition, the focus of the records is not on heavy drinking in isolation but on drinking as an *entreé* into popular culture and recreations. The following examples reveal the pattern of thinking:

> (i) ...Accused of Drinking to Exces and playing At Cards in A publique house And of Singing those Songs which this Church Doe beleeve to bee very disorderly ...
>
> (ii) ... being Acused of being Drunk severall times And swearing And Calling god to damne him If what he said was not true ...
>
> (iii) ... In Drinking too much & keping Carnal Company And especially in Vain & Vocal Singing ...

### (3) Sexual and marital irregularities

The records reveal a conceptual bridge in the collective thinking of the General Baptist churches between alcoholic and sexual misbehaviour:

> ... a very bad report of his being guilty of taking the Lords Name in vain and of Spending a Lords Day Evening in Riot and Drunkeness and committing Fornication ...

The language the clerks used may indicate a difference, as the following two cases of 'fornication' show, in the disciplinary treatment of men and women:

> (i) Dorcas Mighles being Accused of great Iniquity and Evil Conversation wth. other womens Husbands & she Confessing herself Guilty with one of them ... [is excommunicated] Into the World from whence she came ... that the Spirit may be saved in the day of the Lord Jesus Christ.

In that passage, the minute clerk's task was to register the church's horror of moral pollution. In the following excerpt, a promiscuous man is merely suspended from membership:

> (ii) At our Church Meeting the case of David Craply was considered who hath been suspended a long time from the Table of the Lord on Account of Fornication ...

A further sub-division of the General Baptists' recorded disciplinary oversight of sexual and marital matters concerned, as with the Quakers, the avoidance of 'marrying out', and an insistence on endogamy that sociologists of religion regard as a hallmark of the classic religious sect. The next two excerpts show how the general principle of endogamy might be incorporated into church records and how its implementation in a particular case might be minuted:

> At a Church meeting then Held in the Friars Has taken into consideration the Case of members marrying with persons out of Communion and it was agreed That persons so marrying did walk disorderly and were worthy of disgrace ...

In its actual application, the marital disciplinary code had often to be implemented in the form of no more than a requirement of verbal repentance for marriages which had become irreversible *faits accomplis*, and so recorded:

> Bro:John Onewill being this day called to an accot before the Church for having married a Wife out of the fellowship of the Church: ... he was separated from the communion of the said Church untill he shall humble himselfe according to the weight of his offence

### (4) Other disciplinary matters

The records of the General Baptist churches cover a fair spectrum of human nature and human frailty. In one case, for example, an individual steals women's shoes from his father claiming they are for his wife, and 'to Escape the Rigour of the Law' absconds, a case the recording of which the clerk accompanied with marginal reflections from St. Paul's Epistles. The records also reveal some sheer meddling and officiousness: one Canterbury member to be admonished 'not to practice Ringing' and another warned off the 'practice of singing vain songs'. Debt and bankruptcy were further matters for disciplinary action and record.

### Church Doctrine

Enough has been seen of General Baptist records so far to see how important reconciliation and congregational harmony were in the lives of individual churches: thus the Yarmouth church in 1749 regretted a 'Seperation ... thro' discord fallen out in this Church' and rejoiced that 'God in Mercy have given granted [*sic*] us an opportunity to Meeting in unity...'. The church books also devote a certain amount of attention to these themes of consonance and dissonance, with particular reference to doctrine.

Clerks on behalf of their church meetings were certainly likely to record the 'want of the unity of the Spirit which is the Bond of peace' as grounds for serious collective regret, offering various remedies. The church books also evince some desire to avoid contention by playing down doctrine, or at least dogmatism:

> '... to mutually forbear with each other and to allow each other to think for ourselves in matters of Divinity without suspecting each others christianity and without attempting to irritate each others passions on account of difference of sentiment'

How does that kind of stipulation affect the quality of these church books as sources for the doctrinal history of these Dissenting churches? Because of an evident distate for dogmatic discord, individual General Baptist church books cannot be entirely relied upon to chart in detail the great dialectical issues - liberals versus orthodox, rival christologists, unitarians versus trinitarians, evangelicals versus traditionalists - that were dividing this church, and Nonconformity generally, in the 17th and 18th centuries. Often the record books chronicle the doctrinal issues of the day only obliquely, monitoring those controversies in part, though excluding them as topics for discussion, probably since they presented special dangers to already often small congregations. Thus, as we saw, the expressly non-dogmatic 'six principles' had a considerable following and they were incorporated into the titular captions of churches and their record books.

## Membership

This subject occupies a large and important documentary category for the General Baptists, a body with a somewhat sectarian identity and consequently quite distinct membership. Membership totals are a frequent, and for the historian obviously most important, entry in church records.

For individual General Baptist churches themselves, those enumerations of members were so vital that a congregation might open its minute book, after a preamble, with 'An Acoant of The Names of all the Members of the Church ...' . Other churches carried out periodic head-counts, as Dover General Baptists did, for example, in 1682 and 1716, revealing incidentally, a steady erosion of membership numbers over time; later we are provided with a grand total of all those baptised into this congregation between 1674 and 1781.

Other demographic data may include lists of marriages, even though these were normally conducted in parish churches, and also registers of births. These latter may contain valuable socio-historical information when occupations of fathers are given. Obviously, for Baptists, baptismal registers (rather than birth registers) were of primary importance from the point of view of recording church membership. Churches like that of Lutton, Lincs., kept lists of the baptised who had each 'signified his/her desire for Baptism'; some baptisms were recorded in most years with, for instance, 12 in 1772 and 17 in 1778.

The records show that the basic Baptist principle of baptism for mature believers continued generally to be taken seriously, that spouses (especially wives ?) of existing Baptists were baptised, that baptism required a confession of faith and a moral examination from the entrant with the church's approval of his or her membership, and that, in the summer months (but in one case in January), entries might read 'Baptized at River'.

Although in 1744 the important London church of Paul's Alley, Barbican, made believers' baptism optional, that church devoted a considerable amount of space in its record book to its splendid, purpose-built baptistry; these records include arrangement for 'booking' the facilities, catalogues of its elaborate 'Garments furniture and Uttensils', and accounts for its cleaning and general maintenance. A typical early entry in its register of baptisms reads thus:

> N.21 Miriam Bailey Spinster was Baptized by Mr. Lewis Douglas this
> 5 Day of March 1716

Another important General Baptist archival category is that of transfer of members between churches. While the General Baptists did not have the Quakers' well-oiled administrative and secretarial system for facilitating inter-congregational transfers, individual churches did have mechanisms for recording members recommended to them from elsewhere and also for commending migrating church members, especially to the fairly numerous and quite tightly organised London group of congregations. Indeed, a good deal of administrative effort was taken up passing members from congregation to congregation, and though this system would, obviously, break down when a church asked to write a reference did not 'know whom we recommend', at its best it worked quite smoothly. The following is a General Baptist example of what the Quakers would have called a 'removal certificate'; it also establishes ministerial qualifications:

> Beloved Brethren
> the Contents of these lines is to Comend to Your Comunion & Care our
> well beloved Brother in the Lord Thomas Lily of Deale in the said
> County who when he lived here was a Member with us and in full
> Comunion and as far as ever we knew was orderly as become a
> Christian and is well Gifted for the Worke of the Ministry ...

Minute book entries also deal with relations between Baptist congregations on a wider front, for instance, over letting one church's premises to another for rent 'one part each Lord's day'. Merger plans also occupy some space in the records, though a Lutton, Lincs., memorandum informing 'the generations yet to come' of the neighbouring church's blame for the break-down of merger plans may be thought to show some over-estimation of the inherent importance of the scheme. In an earlier period, growth leading to bifurcations could still be a pattern, traced for instance in a Deptford General Baptist minute of 1674 recording the setting up of a separate church at Shad Thames. In contrast, surely no more poignant entry can be found in these minutes than one recording the death of a church. For all its fine library and opulent baptistry, the church in Paul's Alley, Barbican, which W. T. Whitely called the 'most learned, the wealthiest, the most progressive' of the London churches that can be tagged as General Baptist, dwindled in numbers, plagued by disputes over the Trinity, until finally, its lease ran out. On 5 June 1768, with the kind of austere restraint that we might expect from Georgian Nonconformity, the church recorded its own demise:

> Agreed that this church dissolve itself from this day.

## Ministry

The once famous and prosperous Barbican church was certainly one of those urban General Baptist congregations which contributed to the gradual evolution of a salaried ministry. Obviously, this development made of the ministry itself a more significant item of business in the records than it would otherwise have been. Indeed, the emergence of noted General Baptist ministerial talents, the competition of churches, especially in the metropolis, for their services and career moves by pastors all generated a flow of recorded correspondence and financial transactions. The Barbican's relations with the gifted preacher and anti-Deist, James Foster, provide a case in point: Foster was invited by the Pinners' Hall church to take over a vacant pulpit; he wished out of courtesy to consult the Barbican church, which promptly set about looking for 'Some proper Motives' to persuade him to stay with them; this request caused Foster considerable 'affliction', even though he had decided to take up the Pinners' Hall offer and could not combine it with ministry to the Barbican since he was 'against pluralities': the various moves and manoeuvres created a documentary corpus of their own.

Again, as with other churches equipped with a professional ministry, those General Baptist churches, often urban, with a paid ministry found themselves having to give considerably administrative, and hence documentary, attention to additional transactions such as the consequences of pastors' illnesses, including the search for substitutes.

The absence of a stipendiary preaching ministry in individual churches, on the other hand, generated administrative and clerical work of another kind, including the supervision of amateur (and perhaps sometimes amateurish) preachers:

> ... it is fully determined that our Bro. John Smith should lay aside his Preaching amongst us until such a time as the Church shall desire him to resume it ... The reason for our thus desiring him is on Account of near half the Members thinking him not properly Qualified for the work or useful in it.

Whether stipendiary or not, the pivotal ministerial officers in individual General Baptist churches, usually known as elders, were chosen with the utmost care and the procedure recorded, understandably, in a formal, almost notarial, manner:

One Brother Bending having made a confession of faith [this included the General Baptist keynote, 'the General Love of God to all men'] [was inducted] as the Lord's Minister to Serve the Lord and this his Church in the Capacity of an Elder ...

## Finance

In common with the archives of all the Nonconformist churches, those of the General Baptists devote a fair amount of space to church finance. Contributions to church collections were a congregational obligation, enforceable by disciplinary sanctions. Accounts therefore show regular, perhaps monthly, collections, with amounts typically of 6d or 1/- entered against the names of individuals, and much larger sums, of £5 to £20, subscribed by others especially towards the building of new meeting houses. At the Barbican, full accounts show how money and books were donated to build up its extensive, scholarly and wonderfully catholic library.

## Charity

Church records provide an insight into the range of practical services that churches might provide for their members, a lending library at the Barbican, and, at Tunbridge Wells, apparently the provision of a household inventory service for members. However, the most important material service a church could perform for its members was, of course, the provision of charity and welfare, and to this the manuscript records give due space. General Baptist minutes show how deacons presented their accounts of charity moneys they had collected and disbursed, sometimes from legacies, with the sums, usually in shillings, entered against the names of recipients: these names tend to recur over a period, with women's names often predominating, and the sums being expended on rent, funeral expenses and general maintenance. In emergencies, charity sums were sometimes recorded as being transferred from one church to another and, in the period of the penal laws, the churches made loans and paid fines. The rate of payments made in the 1670s and 1680s can provide the historian with a kind of graph of the incidence of persecution. Payments are also recorded to help fund apprenticeships, to sponsor a charity school, for foreign Protestants and in response to government authorised charitable 'briefs', like one launched in 1708 'for the Inhabitants of Iniskilling In Ireland'.

## Building and furnishings

General Baptist church records show a discernible tendency to be dominated by doctrine and discipline, even to the exclusion of more practical concerns. However, a feature found in, or on the premises of, some Baptist churches was a baptismal tank and the installation and maintenance of these were matters of record. A family of wealthy London drapers paid for the Barbican church's baptistry in 1716, the minutes then recording 'that a Publick Baptistory or place for Baptiseing of Adult Persons shall be built...'. Subsequently, as we saw above, the church's minutes carefully recorded the elaborate furnishings and equipment - water pump and stove - to service this elaborate and much cherished facility. For a number of years, the separate Baptistry accounts contain such items as 'To a New Tubb' (3/6d), 'Ten Brass Peggs for hatts', 'Three Combs, Ivory, Box, and horne', and 'one white earthen chamber pott', while one Mrs Haynes was paid 18/-, for Mopps a paile and Washing Linen for the Use of the Baptistory'. A relative absence of detailed attention to architectural plans may indicate a 'puritan' suspicion of aestheticism; however, the financing of building operations may well feature in minutes, as with a list, from Lutton, Lincs., General Baptists, of individuals who had engaged to contribute sums from £5 to £20 towards building a new chapel.

### The form and style of General Baptist Records
A degree of ornamentation is sometimes to be found in these records. The minute book (1711-1721) of the Canterbury General Baptists, for instance, opens with a floridly decorated capital and proceeds, with some formality:

> The Church BOOK
> anno Dom: 1711
>
> This Book is for the use of the Church of Baptist
> Believers of the meeting in the Black Friars in [the]
> City of Canterbury Wherein is to be Recorded the
> agreements orders and appointments of the sd.Church ...

This minute book is in fact somewhat exceptional in its orderly arrangement, with dates of entries, reviews of agreements made in previous meetings, followed by five to eight numbered paragraphs of agenda items, the final proceedings then being signed by about fifteen members (all men). A similar passion for order can be seen  in the Barbican minute book, with its list of members alphabetically arranged and a page-by-page key to dates of their baptisms: 'An Alphabet for the most Ready finding of any Name' (1716). A similarly systematic approach can be seen in the Dover General Baptist Church Book, from 1679, which lists its elders, deacons and members in over seven pages, with about forty names per page and columns giving places of residence. Even so, it must be said that some of these productions, however methodical in their presentation, may be somewhat arid in their contents, with formal and repetitive entries, at least in the mid 18th century, recording the appointments of representatives, transfers of members, collections, and installation of deacons, and a careful avoidance of doctrinal issues. A further point to note with regard to the style of these General Baptist minute books is a terminology that resembles that of the Quakers, including numbered months and the term 'Friends' for members.

### General Baptist research material other than church minute books
A considerable amount of material exists concerning individual ministers. One such, the Lincolnshire General Baptist evangelist, Thomas Grantham (d. 1692), who settled at Norwich in around 1686, earned the distinction, from his grandson, of an actual monument in his church at Whitefriars' Convent, a variation on the kinds of 'document' we are considering in this survey, but one that neatly sums up much of the experience of post-Restoration Dissent:[2]

A memorial
Dedicated to the singular merits of
A faithful confessor and laborious servant of Christ,
Who with true Christian fortitude endured persecution
Through many perils, the loss of friends and substance,
And ten imprisonments for conscience sake,
A man endued with every Christian grace and virtue,
The Rev. Mr. Thomas Grantham,
A learned messenger of the baptized churches,
And pious founder of this church of believers baptized,
Who delivered to King Charles II our declaration of faith,
And also presented to him a remonstrance against persecution,
Both were kindly received and redress of grievances promised.

Is there a hint of ironic comment in that last word of the panegyric?

Thomas Grantham was also the author of a work setting out his Baptist churchmanship and its roots in the early Church, *Christianismus Primitivus* (1678). Verse made easy to memorise was a favoured Nonconformist genre, one of which John Bunyan made good use. The anonymous and 'unspeakably comfortable' manuscript verse interpolations in the copy of Grantham's *Christianismus* in the Norwich City Library provide an example of another kind of source we can use to assemble a picture of General Baptist piety, with its emphases in 'Holyness' and the Sabbath:

Spend the Lord's day in holyness,
At church, at home, within
All that you give the flesh and world
Is your great loss and sin.

A further type of source about ministers, of which Grantham again provides an example, is that of edifying last words, taken down by their auditors:

I came not amongst you for riches or honour, but to preach the Gospell of Jesus Christ, to spend and be spent for your good, both by preaching and printing; as I have told you before submit yourselves to the will of God and to every ordinance of man for the Lord's sake; and give honour to whom honour is due; and walke peaceably with all men ...

**The Particular Baptists: Introduction**

Our identification of the General Baptists as a heterogeneous denomination for purposes of archival study must be modified in the light of the secessionist trends and the later divisive shift towards unitarianism, developments which we considered briefly in our introduction to the section on the General Baptists. Nevertheless, in this present section we shall abide by the traditional distinction of the General Baptists as 'one' form of anti-pedobaptist churchmanship and the Particular Baptists as another.

The origins of the English Particular Baptists can be traced, in London, to the 1630s, when some Calvinistic critics of the Laudian Church of England moved out into a separatist and indeed believers' baptist position, though retaining basically Calvinistic principles about election. The cobbler, John Spilsbury (1593-c.1688), was an early leader and by 1640 his 'Particular', i.e. Calvinistic or predestinarian, Baptists were adopting believers' baptisms by total immersion. Like all the other puritan sects, the Particular Baptists, under the leadership of teachers such as William Kiffin (1616-1701) and Hanserd Knollys (1599?-1691), expanded considerably in the revolutionary decades of the 1640s and 1650s, their mainstream Calvinist doctrines giving some of their ministers a place in the national establishment of religion in the 1650s; this meant that only Particular, and not General, Baptists were ejected from church livings between 1660 and 1662.

By the time of the Restoration, the Particular Baptists had about 130 congregations nationwide, and had been grouping them since the 1650s into regional associations, for example in the West Country and the Midlands. They drew firm lines of demarcation between themselves and non-Calvinistic Baptists and between themselves and pedobaptists. By 1718, the Particular Baptists had 206 congregations in England, with around 40,000 people, heavily located in such areas as Bedfordshire, Bristol, Hertfordshire and the Wiltshire cloth districts. In the late 18th century, the Particular Baptists showed a tendency to modify their strict Calvinism in favour of a more open, mission-orientated theology. They lacked a national assembly in the 18th century, and it is possible that this actually protected them from acute theological factionalism, since there was no central body in which warring parties might struggle for predominance. However, the Particular Baptists developed strong regional structures and to some extent these became fora for doctrinal division over Calvinist tenets in the last 18th and early 19th centuries. Indeed, we shall see how even earlier, at least one informal church record shows such discords arising in an individual congregation.

### Federal Bodies

Although the Particular Baptists held a 'fraternal' board of London ministers, with minutes extant from 1724, their experiment in assembling nationally was suspended between 1689-1692 and 1813. However, the early moves in the direction of a national organisation left a printed, minuted record, for example:

> A Narrative of the proceedings of the General Assembly of divers pastors, and ministring brethren of the Baptized Churches, met together in London, from Septemb. 3 to 12, 1689, from divers parts of England and Wales: owning the doctrines of personal election, and final perseverance, etc. [London, 1689]

After 1692 the focus of Particular Baptist associational life was regional. A characteristic form was the grouping of two or more counties together, as with the Kent and Sussex Association of 'Elders and Ministers' and the venerable Yorkshire and Lancashire Association formed in 1695. The Northamptonshire and Leicestershire Association, formed in 1764 and becoming an important agent for the introduction of a modified Calvinism into the denomination, took in a large swathe of the Midlands. These area bodies sent out copies of a 'Circular Letter' to constituent churches, as with the following example from the Western Association:

> The Elders, Ministers and Messengers of the Several Baptist Churches, meeting .. in association at Wellington, May 29 and 30, 1787, to the several Churches they represent, send Christian salutation etc.

These circulars, usually of about a dozen pages each, had themes such as 'the excellence of the Christian dispensation' (Western Association, 1787), or 'The Privileges and Duties of Gospel Churches considered ...', or 'The Nature and Importance of Repentance' (Yorkshire and Lancashire Association, 1787, 1794). The Yorkshire and Lancashire Association, incidentally, had altered its captions, by 1804, from 'the several Churches they represent' to 'over whom they preside'. Despite such claims, the essential unit in Particular Baptist churchmanship was the individual congregation. Here the vital tasks of administration, ministry and discipline were performed and recorded.

Particular Baptist church records disclose a multifarious range of activities: the appointment of supervisory visitors to the members of congregations; allocating seats; arranging a weekly prayer-meeting or calling for prayers to avert the plague; ensuring the painting of gates and windows; presenting a charity recipient with a shift; or fixing a fast day 'on account of the infectious distemper among the horned cattle'. However, discipline is the single most fully recorded activity

## Records of Particular Baptist Congregations

### Church discipline
This was so important to Particular Baptist churches that record books are heavily taken up with it and one of them, from Frome, opens up without any preamble but with a disciplinary case. For a number of years the record resembles a kind of court roll of disciplinary proceedings, with minutes recording the various routines for dealing with trangressors: 'to send an Admonition ... to be here next month', ... 'to send a 3d Admonition ...', '... to refer .. till next Month ...' - and so on. The record of some whole meetings is taken up solely with a dozen or more disciplinary cases. Cases were kept under review, but not necessarily explored in any great detail unless they reached a piont of particular gravity. A selection of five cases will show something of the procedural and documentary character of Particular Baptist church discipline. The offences vary - astrology, disobedience, drunkenness and so on, and the procedural steps are admonition (sometimes by deputation), attemped reclamation and, if this failed, expulsion:

> (1)   Whereas Roger Kendall is charg'd with Iudicial Astrology, breach of Covenant, & Forgery, Idleness & a bad Conversation otherways in the World: Resolv'd that as the Congn: unanimously agree that things

are abominable Evil & can have no Comunion with him without
Repentance, to send him 2 Messengers wth: an Admonition to require
his attendence next Church Meeting.[3] [The 'messengers' are named]

[Subsequently: 3, 1715]:
Resolved that as Roger Kendall has rejected the Authority of X [Christ]
in his Church & remains after all endeavours impenitent to cut him off to
Divine rule: wch: was accordingly done.

Typically enough, the case of the astrologer had been adjourned twice since its
first introduction before coming to a head in this way.

(2)  [3, 1715]:
Resolved that as Eliza: Oxenham is guilty of an unholy Life, disobedience to her Mother, railing at damning & threatening her, with rejection
of the Church &  departure from it, yet remains impenitent after all
Endeavour to reclaim her, according to the Divine rule that she be cutt
off from this church for the abovenam'd Evils: which was accordingly
done

This case shows how the church might back up parental authority, just as the next
one shows how it insisted upon parental responsibilities. The tone remains
throughout solemn and jurisprudential:

(3)  [3, 1715]:
Agreed to send an Admonition to Stephn: White (being guilty of
drunkenness, danceing or a Companion of such, & not takeing care of
his family but absenting himself from them contrary to divine precept
in that case) ...

The next case, a serious one of misconduct and total defiance of the church,
evokes from the clerk an almost incantatory set of periodic clauses; this
emphatic prose structure can best be seen if we reproduce the minute, not in the
continuous sentence form it has in the original, but in a kind of blank-verse
structure, divided into two sub-sets of lines:

(4)  [6, 1715]:
Resolved that as Jno: King has been guilty of Prophane Curseing &
swearing & an unholy Life,

scandalous in his house,
& troublesome to his Neighbours,
 rejecting the Church,
Insolent in his Carriage,
saying that the Members was Liars,
tht he did not deny the Churchs Charge,
that he did not care if cutt off,
tht he would not be with us,
& after all perswasions impenitent: Saying

if the Church could not have comunion with him,
he would not with them,
that he be Excomunicated ...

Needless to say, not all disciplinary actions conveyed so awesome a sense of
gravity or so transparent a sense of clarity - or even led to an outcome:

(5)  [10. 1721]
Sistr Margery Whitchurch appr:d and nothing could be proved she
denying the burneing the straw or the knowing who did it & that she
provoked him at that time.

In various manifestations, then, normal discipline occupied a good deal of the
administrative time of the Particular Baptists - a classic 'gathered' church - and
a consequent proportion of space in the church books.

**Church ministry**
The moral -and doctrinal - scrutiny of ministers also looms large in Particular
Baptist records. The documentation on the approbation of ministers can indeed
take us deep into the thinking of these Baptists congregations - their love of
homiletic spontaneity and spirit guidance, their desire for the maintenance of
traditional orthodoxy. The formal record of these proceedings might, though, be
used to give permanent form to financial as well as sermonic and doctrinal
requirements from ministers:

[12, 1731]: Agreed that Mr. Hurn appear before the Church only and
speak from a Scripture that we may Judge whither the Lord hath given
him a gift and qualified him for the work of the ministry .. upon
Condition that he comply with the three following propositions
(1) That in appearing before us to speak to us he neither read his matter
nor use notes.
(2) That he stedfastly adheare to the Intrest and truths that hath been
maintained and preached amongst us
(3) That during our pastors life and after his death he shall do nothing
to the prejudice of the Congregatuon in relation to Mr Allen Senrs
money as to the gaining of it from the present trustees who misapplyed
it.

Given that a church had financial as well as doctrinal and spiritual activities, a
clerk might be faced with the challenge of combining in one set of recorded
desiderata monetary as well as religious demands and the result is not necessarily felicitous. As for Mr. Allen's money, which forms part of a whole history of
Baptist testamentary bequests to churches, its disposal itself divided his congregation, reminding us that, while churches might fall out over predestination, they
might also quarrel over a legacy of £200.

Church records may have to deal, simultaneously if not comfortably, with both
spiritual and very practical demands. Spirituality can indeed break through the
press of business in these records, and a church covenant - in the next case from

a time of of persecution - can convey an unmistakeable sense of exaltation. The passage that follows as an example is not punctuated at all, but we might, again, reproduce it not in its original prose shape but in a series of periods suggested by its internal rhythm:

> We who through the Mercy of God and our lord Jesus Christ
> have obtained grace to give ourselves to the Lord and one another
> By the will of God to have communion with one another
>  as Saints in our gospel Fellowship
> do before God our father and our Lord Jesus Christ
> and the holy angels
> agree and promis all of us
> The lord assisting to walk together
>  in this our gospel communion and Fellowship
> as a Church of Jesus Christ
> in Love to the lord
> and to one another ...

That is, obviously, a convenant of union eschewing anything of dogma. Its experiential tone is certainly found in other Particular Baptist church records in the 18th century, as when the Frome church recorded a baptism with an 'account of the dealings of God with [the baptized's] soul ...' However and whatever the emphases on experience and unity, dogma and its divisive potential could not be excluded from these records, or if it was suppressed or ignored in formal records, it might find its way into personal and informal memoranda. This was the case with a twenty-side manuscript recording of a deep theological rift in the important Broadmead church, Bristol, in the year 1733, when that church went over to an entirely Baptist position. The case in question, concerning the Rev. Mr. Harrison, had been 'the Subject of much Conversation', both within and outside the congregation. Mr. Harrison, it appeared, had preached a sermon in which 'he dropt some expressions about conversion which were taken notice of and gave offence to two or three of the Brethren' and after which he was 'attack'd with a great deal of warmth but little good manners', the issue being one central to traditional Calvinistic Baptist soteriology, 'Particular Redemption'.

What do unofficial records like this tell the historian? Perhaps church minute books, those 'official' records which are necessarily the staple fare for the history of Nonconformist congregations in our period, convey a slightly distorted impression, of formal, deferential or basically harmonious relations of congregations to their pastors. Largely absent is any record of those daily and weekly conversations and gossipings on the part of people for whom doctrinal questions had an absorbing interest. That is why a singular source like that of the Harrison case, being a report of eavesdropping and conversational fragments otherwise lost, has such value, since it provides a *tableau vivant* of congregants at odds with both their pastors and riven by theological discord while some theologically literate 'lay' members stood to the defence of threatened Calvinist principles. Mr. Harrison, to the absolute horror of congregants who could not 'bear to have good works preach'd', had told a group of Quakers 'that the reason

of his being dismiss'd ... was because he did not believe God made all the world
[in another account, and more coherently, '3 parts of the world'] to damn them'.

Of course, even the 'formal' records deal with such doctrinal issues, though not
necessarily always with the same conversational immediacy as the private report
of the Harrison case. Thus, the Baptist documentary sample that we have just
been considering, takes us deep into scenes of clerical and lay life in an 18th-
century congregation, some of whose members were trying to cling on to basic
Calvinistic certainties - originally hallmarks of Particular Baptist churchmanship and now assailed by a revisionist preacher.

### Buildings and furnishings
Particular Baptist archival materials concerned with buildings include documents transferring to trustee church members existing properties to be converted
for use as chapels; an example concerns the transfer of property to the Cloughold,
Lancs., Particular Baptists:[4]

> Mr Robert Litchford, formerly of Blakely, in the County of Lancaster,
> Gentleman, on the 11th of February, 1705, surrendered into the hands of
> the Lord and Lady of the Manor of Accrington all that edifice or building
> standing within Cloughfold, in the said Manor, ... to the use of and behoof
> of Messrs. Richard Holden [and three others], who shall at all times for
> ever stand and be heired of the said edifice, for the use and benefit of all
> such Protestant Dissenters, called Anabaptists or Independents, within
> the Forest of Rossendale ..., when the same shall be made fit and commo
> dious for a chapel or meeting house.

As for the erection of a purpose-built chapel, records of the Particular Baptist
church at Bacup, Lancs., show some of the typical stages as they were
documented. First, an appeal for funds (1746):[5]

> Friends and Brethren, - We the members of the Church at Bacup,...being
> obliged to meet in houses, and our congregation being so large, that not
> one-half can have the opportunity to hear ... We have at last thought of
> building a meeting house, but our circumstances in the worldare forbid
> ding, many of us being poor. We therefore desire you would take these
> things into consideration, and freely bestow some charity to assist in so
> great a work as building a convenient meeting place. The method we
> propose with respect to the building is to give freely without one having
> more title therein than another, intending to let the seats, and the money
> raised to be for the support of the minister, ...

Subsequent stages included a list of the main subscribers (14 men and one
woman in this case), with the amounts, from 10/- to £10, subscribed. Accounts
are entered thus:

To RICHARD LORD,                                      Dr.
1746

July 22. To 1 day's work at ground work ...      11d
"    23.    ½ a day, 1 horse and self leading stone 10½d...
1746
Aug. 16. Paid to Wm. Roberts for 3 dinners and drink 10d

Churches also recorded their care of their premises:[7]

Oct. 1, 1779. The Chh. hath this day agreed to grant James Bentley
10/- p. year for his care of the chapell.

They raised sums for minor works:

Subscriptions in order to pay off the expenses of gates and other work
done about the Chapell, Oct: 4, 1788

Congregations also carefully embellished their meeting houses:

November 27, 1806. -- Many hearers of the word with us having a desire
to have a clock in the chapel, aske the Chh. if they will grant it. The price
will be perhaps £5 5s or 10s. One man has promised £1 or £1 1s.
November 29, 1806. Clock for chapel alowed.

**Research material other than church minutes**
Hymns can be an important source for our understanding of the religious
thinking and feeling of a church. The Particular Baptist hymnodist Edward Triv-
ett, pastor at Worstead, Norfolk, between 1741 and 1792, had printed for his
church's use hymns of deep evangelical feeling:[8]

View Jesus on the painful tree,
What love! What vast provision be;
His flesh is meat, most rich indeed,
His blood such drink as sinners need.
With Christ is found a full supply,
We eat and drink abundantly;
His body broke gives life to those
Who pardon seek and with Him close.

One of the greatest figures in English religious life and history, John Bunyan, as
a Calvinist and one who had undergone believer's baptism, was a Particular
Baptist, though he preferred the title 'Christian' to any restrictive sectarian label.
Bunyan's voluminous writings, 60 separate works in 60 years of life, take us
deep into Particular Baptist thought, especially its insistence on justification by
faith alone and predestination. In such works as *A Confession of Faith and a
Reason of my Practice* (1672), *Difference in Judgment About Water Baptism No
Bar To Communion* (1673), and *Peaceable Principles and True* (1674), Bunyan
argued for latitude within the sect over the strict necessity for an actual sacrament
of adult 'Water Baptism'.

## Notes to Chapter 2

1.  Watts, *The Dissenters*, pp. 49-50, 70-1, 112, 114, 160, 166, 232-3, 268-9, 283-4, 298, 30, 373, 455-6, 465.

2.  The following excerpts are from Charles Boardman Jewson, *The Baptists in Norfolk*, (London, n.d.), pp. 29, 33-4, 36.

3.  'Judicial astrology' involved the use of horoscopes for the purpose of divining and seeking answers to specific and personal questions. Religious opinion tended to consider it particularly reprehensible. I am indebted for this information to Dr S. P. Pumfrey.

4.  Jones Parry, History of *Cloughold Baptist Church*, p. 145.

5.  Frederick Overend, *History of the Ebenezer Baptist Church Bacup*, (London, 1912) pp. 145-6.

6.  *Ibid.*, p. 147.

7.  For the following excerpts, *ibid.*, p. 171, 174, 180-1.

8.  Jewson, , p. 47, *Baptists in Norfolk*

## Sources for Chapter 2

Excerpts of manuscript material in this chapter come from General and Particular Baptist minute books, some of them in microfilm form, in D.W.L.: Great Yarmouth General Baptist Minutes 1703-1771; Church Book of Dover Unitarian (General Baptist) Church from 1679; General Baptist Churches in and about East Kent, First Minute Book; Canterbury (General Baptist) Church Book, 1663-1695; Church Book of Dover Baptists 1668-1675; Deptford General Baptist Chapel, Minutes, volume 1, 1674-1710; Lutton, Lincs., General Baptist Church Book; Canterbury General Baptist Church Book 1711-1721; A Journal of the Proceedings at the Quarterly Meeting of ... General Baptist churches of East Kent, 1780-7; Deptford General Baptists' Register 1785-1821 (transcript); London Barbican General Baptists' Church Book; Tunbridge Wells General Baptists' Deacons' Book, 1697-1744; Particular Baptist Church, Frome; Hitchin Particular Baptist Records (transcript); Walter Wilson MS, L7.

In print, W. T. Whitley, *Minutes of the General Assembly of the General Baptist Churches in England, With Kindred Records* (2 vols, London, 1909) forms an encyclopaedic collection. Also in print, though covering a period before this survey commences, is B. R. White, ed., *Association Records of the Particular Baptists of England, Wales and Ireland to 1660* (3 vols., 1971-4). An account of, and some records from, a local associational structures are available in Frank Buffard, *Kent and Sussex Baptist Associations* (Faversham, Kent, n.d.), Local church records in print include, *The Records of a Church of Christ in Bristol* edited by B. Hayden for the Bristol Record Society, 1974; E. B. Underhill's edition of *Records of the Churches of Christ Gathered at Fenstanton, Hexham and Warboys, 1640-1720*, for the Hanserd Knollys Soc., 1854; and *The Church Book of Ford, Cuddington and Amersham*, edited for the Baptist Historical Society, 1912. See also C. B. Jewson, *The Baptists of Norfolk*, (London, 1957); Frederick Overend, *History of Ebenezer Baptist Church Bacup* , (London, 1912) and Jones Parry, *History of Cloughold Baptist Church.* Two important recent additions are *English Baptist Records 2 Church Book: St.Andrew's Street Baptist Church, Cambridge,* and *English Baptist Records 3 Association Life of the Particular Baptists of Northern England* , (Baptist Historical Society, 1991).

Some helpful guidance on 'Baptist Church Records' is given by A. H. J. Baines in *Archives*, v (1961), pp. 7-8. The *Transactions of the Baptist Historical Society* were merged, from 1922, with the *Baptist Quarterly.* A complete edition of Bunyan's works is in progress from the Clarendon Press , Oxford and there also exists a three volume edition of the complete works of John Bunyan by George Offor (1865).

Some selected Baptist sources at various repositories include:

For Kent: Dover Baptist Church Minutes, 1778-1814, in Kent County Archives Office, Maidstone.

For Cornwall: Webber St., Falmouth, (Particular) Baptist records, dates unknown, at Falmouth Baptist Church; Helston (Particular) Baptists' Baptism or Births Registers, 1805-1837, in the P.R.O.; Kenwyn (nr. Truro) (Particular) Baptists' Minutes, 1764-1840, at Falmouth Baptist Church; Redruth (Particular) Baptist Chapel Records from 1801, at Redruth Baptist Church.

For Devon: Barnstaple (Particular) Baptist Minute Books from 1817, at Barnstaple Solicitors; Dartmouth (Particular) Baptist Records from 1786, at Dartmouth Baptist Church; Exeter (Particular) Baptists' Birth or Baptisms Records, 1775-1837, and Burials, 1785-1837, at the P.R.O.; Great Torrington New St. (Particular) Baptist Minute Books from 1820, at Great Torrington New St. Baptist Church; Kentisbeare (Particular) Baptist Records, from 1816, at the Kentisbeare, Sainthill, Baptist Church; Plymouth, Old George St., (Particular) Baptists' Births or Baptisms Registers, 1787-1837 and Burials, 1787-1837, at the P.R.O.; Tiverton (Particular) Baptists' Births or Baptisms, 1767-1837, and Burials, 1816-1837, at the P.R.O., and early records, at Tiverton Baptist Church.

For Dorset: Lyme Regis (Particular) Baptist Minute Book, 1653, at Lyme Regis Baptist Church.

For Somerset: Wellington Baptists' births, 1781,at the P.R.O.; Chard Baptists' Minute Book, 1653, at the Somerset Record Office, Taunton.

For Essex: Burnham Baptists' Accounts, 1695-1786, and Minutes, 1701-41, in Essex Record Office, Chelmsford.

Archival material on individual Baptists includes: in the Suffolk Record Office, Bury St. Edmunds: Correspondence and Diaries (1825-33) of Cornelius Elven (1797-1873), the Suffolk Baptist minister; in The Baptist Missionary Society, London, correspondence of the Northants minister and secretary of the Baptist Missionary Society, Andrew Fuller (1754-1815).

# CHAPTER III

## RECORDS OF THE INDEPENDENT CHURCHES

### Introduction

The Independency of our period has some traceable links back to Elizabethan and Jacobean Protestant religious dissidence, and especially to a modified form of separatism pioneered under James I by Henry Jacob (1563-1624). The more immediate origins of Independency can be identified in a group of strongly Calvinist ministers reacting against the Laudian Church of England in the 1630s. A cohort of former anti-Laudian exiles in the Netherlands, William Bridge (c.1600-1670), Jeremiah Burroughs (c.1600-1676), Thomas Goodwin (1600-1680), Philip Nye (1596-1672) and Sidrach Simpson (c.1600-1655) emerged in the mid-1640s in the body set up by Parliament to reform the nation's religious life, the Westminster Assembly of Divines. These five signatories of the *Apologeticall Narration* of 1644 were the original clerical nucleus of what had already become known as Independency. In the course of the 1640s, the terms 'Independent' and 'Independency' were used, loosely, to denote both secessionist 'gathered' churchmanship and also a leaning towards a version of the 'New England way' of congregations of 'visible saints' existing within a framework of parochial, state-supported church life. Moderate, congregational Independency represented a position of some delicacy and subtlety between the social comprehensiveness and authoritarianism thought to characterise the Presbyterians and the more atomised and frankly secessionist outlook of the Separatists.

The Independents were closely associated with the acceleration of millenarian expectations in the 1640s and 1650s, and the seminal millenarian work, *A Glimpse of Syons Glory*, was written by an Independent minister. The Independents' sense of expectation of 'godly rule' was expressed in overall support for the Republic after 1649, and Independents took an important role in the broad-based national church of the 1650s, though combining this with a more selective 'gathered' church membership.

The complexities and even ambiguities of the Independency of the 1650s, whether it represented a social churchmanship under the umbrella of a national establishment of religion or a more separatist option, were largely resolved after the Restoration, when the Independent presence in the national Church was expunged between 1660 and 1662. Following the ejections of the latter year, both Presbyterians and Independents were forced towards a shared ecclesiological position of voluntary churchmanship, and their increasingly close collaboration climaxed in the 'Happy Union' of 1691. However, that fusion failed to destroy, indeed it re-awoke, some very real basic differences between the Presbyterian and Independent outlooks, and the ultra-Calvinistic bedrock Independency of Richard Davis (1658-1714) in the early 1690s brought out some of the differences, splitting the Happy Union by the mid-1690s, though its spirit, structures and aspirations survived in some regions.

By 1718, the Independents, though the second largest group of Nonconformists after the Presbyterians, lagged way behind them in terms of numbers (about 60,000 to the Presbyterians' c.180,000), and hardly amounted to more than 1% of the overall population, with pockets of strength in areas like mid-Anglia. In the course of the 18th century, Independency largely (though not entirely) avoided the theological revisionism that the Presbyterians experienced. Indeed, Independency accrued strength, especially in the North, not only because Presbyterian congregations, repelled by unitarian trends, were attracted to Independency's more unsullied Calvinism but because some Calvinistic forms of the Evangelical Revival created new Independent clusters.[1]

The primacy of the individual congregation in Independency gave it an overall simplicity of organisational structure, though it did evolve some area bodies. Independents also took part in supra-denominational institutions such as the committee of the Three Denominations, and also participated, alongside those of a Presbyterian persuasion, in area joint bodies such as the United Brethren in Devon and Cornwall, and other similar fora, especially in the 1690s, in Yorkshire, Cheshire and Lancashire. However, after the Savoy Conference in 1658, attempts to give Independency a national associational form did not come to fruition until after the end of the period of this survey. Therefore, the true focus of Independent life and organisation was the particular congregation and it is with the records of these that we shall chiefly be concerned in this chapter.[1]

## Church convenants
Since the individual congregation was the primary unit, much depended on its self-awareness, doctrinal consensus, fellowship, discipline and the quality of its ministry. The importance and coherence of the particular congregation as the essential unit of the church were expressed typically in church covenants, the idea of the convenant being deeply embedded in the Reformed consciousness that formed Independency. These convenants, or contracts, between the members, often form preambles to church record books, and are sometimes accompanied by a profession of faith, of varying degrees of precision. However, minute theological definition was as often as not eschewed in these agreements, since it might conflict with the basic Independent emphasis on fellowship and tolerance.

Going back to the Elizabethan pre-history of Independency, a church covenant was a solemn, recorded, renewable foundation document of a gathered community of worship, a binding indenture pledging its subscribers' exclusive allegiance to the church and to acceptance of its discipline; ultimately, a convenant was also a written agreement between the members and God, committing them to 'walk in His ways', to 'walk in the Faith and Order of the Gospel', in return for His blessings. The following example may be taken as typical of the genre, not least in the solemnity of its phrasing:

> We do Covenant or Agree, in the Presence of God... to walk together
> in All the Ordinances of the Lord Jesus, so far as the same are made
> clear unto us; Indeavouring the Advancement of the Glory of our
> Father, the Subjection of our Wills to the Will of our Redeemer, & the
> Mutual Edification, each of other, in his most holy faith & Fear

A covenant declaration may be accompanied by a profession of the faith that brought the covenanting parties together and a credal profession may evince considerable theological sophistication. This need not surprise us. The nuclei of the membership of Independent churches were made up, typically, of fairly small numbers of committed Christians who took religious doctrine seriously and who were alert to doctrinal nuances. Occasionally, a profession of faith may show signs of composition by a trained theologian versed in traditional scholastic terminology:

> [God is] One in Essence, though yet distinguished by Relative Properties into Three Persons... three several ways of Subsistence ...

On the whole, and certainly until the mid-18th century, the Independents fully subscribed to orthodox Calvinist theology, especially its elective or predestination approach to salvation. This may feature in the records, and be expressed with considerable emphasis:

> God... from all Eternity forseeing the miserable Defection of Man, did purpose & decree ... to advance ... the Glory of his ... Grace, in the Recovery of Some of those persons which were ... lost through Adam's Sin ... [Christ] paid the price ... of Salvation for all the Elect of God ... is become Author of Life ... only to so many as believe ... And that ... Faith ... is ... special and proper Gift of God given peculiarly to the Elect

We have already seen, from the case of the General Baptists, that church records, especially in prefatory sections, may be used to make statements of theological position. The difference is, of course, that the doctrinal stances - in the one case Arminian, in the other predestinarian - are diametricaly opposed. It was entirely appropriate to link a written covenant with a written creed as the identifying hallmarks of a church, the badge of its distinctive credal personality. However, since an over-elaborate creed might run counter to the unitive purposes of church covenants, these credal statements needed to be written with some skill and delicacy. Their essential point was to assert the basic consensual principles - unitarian, elective - that were supposed to command general assent and maintain fellowship in Independent churches:

> ...in matters dubious ... we are to yield, each to others, all Christian Forbearance that may stand with our walking orderly in Love, & inoffensively to a Brother's Conscience.

Such entries were designed to avert anticipated doctrinal discord. Records from some Independent churches suggest that, although the Independents largely avoided dogmatic schisms nationally, local congregations were at least threatened by such divisions - and sought to avoid them as, the General Baptists had, by recourse to the apparent simplicities of Scripture:

> ... in all matters of controversy, we will be determined by the sole authority of the Bible ...

## Church history

Church covenants and other prefatory documents may contain surveys of the histories of congregations, how they came together, what vicissitudes they had faced, and the all-important question of a church's ministry; the church at Southwold, Suffolk recalled that it had not come together, but that it had been 'formed' by its first pastor, George Wiggett. Wattisfield church, Suffolk, in contrast, recounted its spontaneous formation without pastoral guidance, but with many years of difficulty and an almost providential rescue it was formed :

> after the Congregational Way ... being few in number, & without a Pastor, ... travelled for above 23 years through many Difficulties, passed under Changes of times, suffered by Death of Members, but most of all endangered by Intestine Divisions, but ... delivered from threatened Ruin, began to revive & flourish ... though it was a suffering Day with others ...

Independent church records sometimes contain vital information on events outside the churches and their reactions to them. Sometimes, as in the last excerpt, the information is lightly coded: 'Changes of times', 'a suffering Day' are unmistakable references to English history after 1660.

The 'historical' material in these minute books may also contain important data about membership and numbers. Statistics are given, frequently in the form of page lists of original members and subsequent entrants, by date of entry. For instance, Wattisfield's records show in 1678 a pastor, two members of the congregation of the mid-1650s, with nine men and twelve women members joining thereafter. Southwold Independent church counted a total of ten founder members in 1748, six of them women, and a subsequent healthy growth rate of between two and nine new entrants a year, though some years had no new admissions. Evidence of a preponderance of women is emphatically born out at Great Yarmouth, where, for example, of ten new entrants in September 1659, eight were women, while all four new members in August 1660 were women, and three out of four in December.

Numerical indices were obviously watched closely and minuted carefully, and heavy or rapid decrease caused alarm, so that minutes might record the elders asking searching questions about the graces through which a church was built up and the sins which 'chiefly tend unto Unchurching or removing of the Candlesticks...'.

## Church ministry

Independency took its rise in the 1640s from the dissidence expressed by a group of ordained ministers in the Westminster Assembly of Divines. In its subsequent development, the denomination placed heavy emphasis on the value of ministry. The congregation at large was, of course, the key unit of the church, but its main ordained pastoral minister was its cynosure. He led worship and normally delivered the expositions and sermons which were the mainstays of Independent communal worship. Ministers were elected by congregations, though into the early 18th century there could still be some disagreement over the relative roles of congregations and of existing ministers. A salaried minister in a congregation was the norm, and though the amounts paid varied widely between congregations and regions, the general standard was modest. It should be noted that professional ministry was not the only option, and that Independency reserved a place for preachers 'fitted by the Holy Ghost'.

One indication of the high value that congregations put upon their ministers is the appearance of ministerial biographies and obituaries in church books. For example, the Wattisfield church recorded a biography of its important second minister, Edmund Whincop, Cambridge graduate, medical man and schoolmaster, who was converted, became an Independent minister and was not only ejected in 1662 but imprisoned 'merely upon suspicion of keeping private worship'. Whincop was called to the pastorate in 1678 and, though we may imagine that Wattisfield's twenty or so congregants faced considerable difficulty in supporting him financially, the church gained members in his time, an increase marked with a day of 'Solemn Thanksgiving'. Obituaries also featured:

> November 12th 1782 Died, The Revd. Mr. Jas. Webb aged 74 -- He had been 24½ years Pastor of the Church in Fetter Lane -- He was laid aside from his work about six weeks previous to his death which was the effect of Nature being worn out ... Mr. Winter preach'd the funeral Discourse to a crowded Auditory from Psal 23 & 4th Verse -- Tho' I walk thro' the Valley of the shadow of death ...

**The choice, call and inauguration of ministers**
Following on the death, resignation or retirement of a pastor, an elaborate and fully documented set of procedures came into operation, giving effect to the Independents' cherished principle that the individual church was equipped 'with Power to Elect ... all her own Officers'. The following excerpts[2] provide examples of the procedural steps and the documentation involved in the making of a momentous choice:

In the opening moves, the men members of the congregation met to consider a proposal

> The Brethren met at the Globe in Hatton Garden to consult with each other respecting an Invitation to Dr. Davis to accept the Pastoral Office .. He was pretty generally approved of - the chief objection was his distance & engagements at the Academy.

This is the first mention of Davis as a prospective minister, and the record is silent on the original source of this initiative. However, this proposal was next turned into a formal motion put to a specially convened church meeting. Unanimity rather than majority was sought, if possible:

> That the Rev.d Dr. Davies [sic] is an able faithful Minister of the Gospel and is a fit & proper Person to fill up the Pastoral Office of this Church -- To the former part of the resolution none wd. have objected but all were not willing to assent to the whole --

On a division 8 hands were held up for the Motion & 2 against it -- After
a good deal of conversation a motion was made ... that the further consideration of the business be postponed.

If complete unanimity was unattainable, the wishes of the overwhelming
majority prevailed, and a formal invitation to the church's ministry, the 'call',
was penned and signed. This 'call' of a new minister, probably the most
important single event in the life of an Independent church, involving the
binding mutual commitment of pastor and congregation, was accompanied by
extensive documentation.[3] In the Fetter Lane case, difficulties over Dr Davis's
transfer had to be resolved, then Davis sent a letter of acceptance which was read
and entered into the record along with his release from his church at Abergav-
enny, he and his wife were made members of Fetter Lane, the church verbally
renewed its call to him in person, he accepted 'in a short speech', and the
chairman of the meeting on behalf of the church promised 'all due Affection,
Submission & Obedience unto him as their Pastor in the Lord'. The documentation throughout conveys an unmistakeable impression of careful deliberation,
courtesy, decorum and plain dealing.

Finally, arrangements could be recorded for the new minister's inauguration and
a number of congregations invited to send ministers and emissaries, not to
participate in an ordination but 'to observe our Order'; a solemn induction
proceeded with a prayer, a 'short Discourse on the nature of Gospel Churches &
their duties', a formal enquiry about the ordinand, a full-length sermon, another
prayer and the conclusion of the session by the new minister. The laying on of
hands is not mentioned. From Fetter Lane, a party of eighty eight then went off
to a, no doubt well-deserved, dinner at the 'Pauls head tavern, Cateaton Street'.
As far as the church's records are concerned, that was the end of the affair.
However, if a resignation was required, as when at Fetter Lane Dr Davis fell ill
and could no longer preach or administer the Sacrament , further documentation
was called for, including notice of retirement and the church's acceptance
thereof:

> Permit us Revd. Sir to present our sincere & affectionate thanks to those
> eminent services we have for many years recd. from you ... many of us
> have reason to bless the Lord that he sent you among us ... a connection
> which we believe was formed under Divine leadings, & attended with
> a Blessing...

One of the most noticeable distinguishing marks of Independency was congregational choice of 'officers' - not just full-time pastors and other preachers but
elders and deacons to administer discipline and poor relief, help manage the
church and generally assist with its ministry. The records of the Great Yarmouth
church provide further examples of the procedures used by Independents in
church elections,[4] including those for the pastorate itself. Firstly, at the end of a
day of prayer and humiliation, one of the brethren reminded the church of its
responsibility to choose officers and ministers. Secondly, the church members
made an initial selection of two officers, a pastor and a 'teaching elder', and
asked the nominees to take this into consideration as a call. Then, six or seven

months after the first initiative, the two accepted their calls at a meeting of 'brethren and sisters'. Another three months later, in a protracted ceremony, the church solemnly inducted two new ministerial officers and then renewed its covenant at the end of a day of 'solemn humiliation'. Sometimes congregational voting figures for elections are recorded. In 1784, for example, the Fetter Lane church held a ballot for two deacons, the leading candidates getting 19 and 15 votes each and eight other men obtaining between one and nine votes apiece.

As we have seen, the individual congregation was the basic autonomous union of Independent government and of ministerial choice. This did not mean that the particular congregation was entirely isolated, and the records of Independency show signs of inter-congregational activity. In earlier days, federal bodies might still operate on the county level, if only as a way of of monitoring a tense political situation; thus in November 1659 the Yarmouth church received a letter from Independency's most influential minister, John Owen, 'desiring a meeting of the Churches in Norfolke', the Yarmouth church deputing two members to attend[5]. Although a national body was not revived until the 19th century, regional associations of ministers were resumed in East Anglia from the mid-18th century, and from the 1780s over 20 county associations, directed at missionary evangelisation, arose in different parts of the country.

The records of individual Independent churches also throw light on the complex relations, practical and theoretical, between two main wings of the Anglo-Calvinist tradition, Independency and Presbyterianism. After 1662, any such hard-and-fast distinctions between Independent and Presbyterian became less real (though they were taken seriously) since Presbyterians forced out of the Church of England were pushed towards a Dissenting position and the individual Presbyterian congregation was coming to resemble an Independent church, though with more ministerial authority, while Independency itself became more overtly separatist. Nevertheless, despite frequent quite successful moves in the direction of Presbyterian-Independent accord, principles of church government could still be doctrinally divisive. Thus the Great Yarmouth church minuted its refusal to chose as its pastor a Scot, Mr Frazor, because of his 'Presbyterian principalls'.[6]

The records also provide some insights into relations with other denominations, which could be hostile, especially with the Quakers, far removed as they seemed to be from Independency's relative social conservatism and Calvinist theology:

> It is our desire that countenance be not given nor trust reposed in the hands of Quakers they being persons of such principalls as are destructive to the Gospel & Inconsistant with the peace of civill Societies.

### Church membership
Independent church books are important sources for information about church membership, and we have already seen something of the data they provide on membership numbers. They also yield information on (1) admission procedures; (2) levels of membership; (3) transfers of members; and (4) resignations of membership.

### (1) Admission procedures

Independents held that an important prerogative of the individual church was the power of 'receiving in and casting out'; therefore, their records may sometimes reveal how prospective entrants were required to provide something along the lines of 'an account of their Competency in the Knowledge of Christianity to the Pastor and of their sober life and Conversation...'. There was a tendency not to demand prohibitively high standards of articulateness, experiential originality, doctrinal awareness or moral perfection from new entrants and to allow them to testify to the pastor alone, rather than to the whole congregation, interviews that were not necessarily matters of record.

### (2) Levels of membership

Independency seems to have had a kind of two-tier affiliation, of full members and attenders or 'hearers'. The numerical divergence between the two categories could be quite glaring. Indeed, when we read of such figures as 1,000 congregants at Great Yarmouth in the post-Restoration period, we should bear in mind that they include all those present at a meeting for worship, full members as well as the outer ring of worshippers. At Ipswich in *c.*1720, the Independent church had 120 members but about 500 hearers; at Kettering there were 112 members but over 700 hearers.[7] Independency thus preserved something of the interpenetration it had had during the 1640s and 1650s with the wider world of the parishes, and an Independent congregation might be simultaneously both a gathered church and a more inclusive assembly. An aspect of this acceptance of an outer periphery of membership may have been some tolerance of Occasional Conformity with the Church of England, as suggested in a Fetter Lane schedule of 11 'Occasional Communicants who statedly sit down with the Church'.

### (3) Transfer of members

Like the General Baptists and, more elaborately, the Quakers, the Independents evolved some documentary procedures for transferring members from one congregation to another, with certification of a member's standing. The procedure, such as it was, affords a reminder that Independent churches were not autonomous in the sense of being isolated:

> We need not to write anything by way of Commendation ... his Praise is in the Churches. Our great Loss will be ... your great Gain, in which we shall rejoice.

Obviously, such certificates were all the more appropriate for members involved in any way in church ministry.

### (4) Resignations of membership

Apart from losses of members caused by disciplinary expulsions (including excommunication for non-attendance), archives of Independent churches record losses of members, especially to other branches of Nonconformity. Such losses might take one of two forms: (a) group secessions, as when Fetter Lane church recorded that two members had left '& become a Baptist Church' and (b) individual departures for other churches, as in a case from Norwich:

Haveing a sister fallen from them to Quakerism they desired the
advice of the Churches how to deale with her.

## Church Discipline

The inner nucleus at least of an Independent congregation formed a kind of
'gathered church', and took discipline seriously. It was indeed an inescapable
responsibility of the church and its successive steps were 'Admonition of the
Censures, to wit, Admonition both private & public, [and] Excommunication ...
. [In] the Purest Churches many Graceless Spirits & Cunning Hypocrites may...
crowd in ... and if upon Discovery by clear Evidence that Church does not Labour
to purge out such ... from amongst them ... it is that Church's sin'. Given its
centrality in the maintenance of the integrity of at least a church's inner core, it
is not surprising that discipline makes up the biggest single item in the
documentary corpus of the Independent churches in our period. Though it is true
that different congregations in different parts of the country put varying degrees
of emphasis on discipline, virtually all of them spent at least some time on this
matter, and even the Fetter Lane congregation, sometimes regarded as notably
liberal in its discipline, set aside, as we shall see, some space in its deliberations
and records for this activity.

The main disciplinary infractions recorded in the documentary sources are: (1)
non-attendance and lapse of membership; (2) bankruptcy; (3) drink; and (4)
doctrinal deviations. We shall also consider documentary sources for procedures
of reconciliation.

### (1) Non-attendance

As with the General Baptists, the Independents' procedure for dealing with this
offence amounted in effect to the church formally endorsing the individual's decision to withdraw. For example, the church book of the Old (Independent)
Meeting, Norwich, records how two individuals who had 'walked disorderly by
their Leaving of Communion with the Church for a Long tyme' 'were declared
to be no members of the Church any Longer the Church withdrawing from them
as they had down before from the Church'.

### (2) Bankruptcy

Independent congregations shared attitudes that were widespread in Nonconformity on this topic. While bankruptcy in itself was not considered necessarily
reprehensible, it was a matter for censure and discipline if brought about by
personal extravagance or excessive risk taking. A businessman's bankruptcy
harmed his creditors and the good name of his church. Cases coming before the
Fetter Lane Independent church, in the heart of a commercial and financial
community in the 1780s, illustrate some of these considerations and the often
protracted procedures for the ecclesiastical discipline over bankruptcy.

A case might begin with an unfavourable report by a church member; claims that
a bankrupt was the victim himself of bad debts might be heard quite sympatheti-
cally but any suspicion of fraud on the part of the bankrupt aroused a mood of
acute censure. Deacons monitored cases but all full church members were

involved in deciding the outcome; numerous sessions might have to be held, especially if financial details were complex; and suspension or expulsion for what was considered the moral infraction of avoidable bankruptcy might lead to considerable bitterness on the part of those disciplined and their supporters: in one case, there was an abrupt withdrawal from the church by a bankrupt's son and daughter in protest at 'the unkind treatment their father had received'.

### (3) Drink

As with most other Nonconformist churches, this was a recurrent topic in Independent church books. Heavy drinking was in itself a matter for censure: for example, the Norwich church censured a member who 'had gown on in the sin of dronkennesse for many years...'. The records also show how drinking was linked in disciplinary proceedings with illicit popular pastimes and with indiscriminate gregariousness, for example on the part of one who 'had for a Long tyme been a frequenter of alehouses and given there to play at dice with proffan psons'.

### (4) Doctrinal deviations

Recorded disciplinary action for doctrinal dissidence was not frequent and concerned eccentricities regarded as particularly egregious, as with a Yarmouth member in 1690 whose church was 'Informed that his Judgement is against Baptizing Infants and against singing of psalmes with the Multitude ... upon which the Church denyed him Societie with us'. Significantly, disciplinary action enters the record here in an area not so much of more or less abstract private conviction but in a practical sphere where the church's composition and worship were involved.

### Procedures for reconciliation

Well developed and well documented mechanisms existed in Independent churches for the submission and reconciliation of individuals who had been subject to disciplinary suspensions and expulsions. Such submissions were in fact regarded as the successful completion of the disciplinary process and might therefore be accompanied 'with a great deale of seeming brokennesse of hearte, which did much reffresh the brethren and sisters...'. Some cases of reconciliation were perfectly straightforward and recorded accordingly: in Fetter Lane a Mr Wingfield, formerly a member, had been expelled for absenteeism but negotiations had led to his being 're-admitted to the fellowship of the Church'. Offences regarded as more serious than absenteeism obviously required more exigent conditions for re-admission and the minute of the church meeting recording the conditions should be seen as a clear, written specification of what was required. A Great Yarmouth member who had repented his earlier 'Uncleanness' had his re-entry into the church made conditional upon his meeting five onerous terms, amounting to a commitment on his part to be particularly 'strickt and diligent' so as not to 'grieve the spirits of those that are good'. Reconciliation might also be partial and graduated, in a kind of phased forgiveness monitored over more than one church meeting; thus it was with one of the Yarmouth congregation's many seamen members who admitted his heavy drinking, which acknowledgement 'was accepted in part' and he was 'desired when he found his heart more broken to come and express it to the Church'.

The records also candidly minuted those cases in which the exercise of discipline underwent serious breakdowns and was rejected, when reconciliation emphatically did not function: a woman member of Great Yarmouth church, for instance, accused of 'scandalous walking', was summoned to a hearing, arrived, claimed she was falsely accused, contemptuously turned her back on her accusers, and later returned 'Justifying herself and condemning the Church', which seemed left with little choice but to 'withdraw' from her.

### Fellowship
We have already seen that in matters ranging from the retirement of ailing ministers to the readmission of penitent members, a marked feature of Independent church records is a certain emotionality and a strong personal dimension. A group of church book entries giving obituary notices of members of a church further illustrates this feature:[9] A widow, Mrs. Christian Osborn, is recalled - a founder member who died at the age of 86 and 'in much Love to the Ordinances, and in her whole Conversation as became the Gospel'. Ann Kerry had given 'a good Testimony of a Gracious Spirit, good Experience, with an Holy Converstion in an evil World & backsliding day'. John Serles had been 'a faithful brother, & beloved for his simplicity & Godly Sincerity ...'

### Church Management
Financial matters, predictably, loom large in the recorded proceedings of Independency, with its trained and salaried ministry. Collections, of which detailed accounts were recorded, were an indispensable lifeblood, including those towards the Independent Fund, a levy to assist students for the ministry and poor congregations and their ministers: to this the wealthy Fetter Lane congregation contributed generous sums, going as high as £128 in 1807. Internal church charity made heavy demands on certain congregations. In 1667, for instance, the Norwich Church Book recorded a collection 'for the poor raysed extraordinary', though even on this matter characteristic Independent procedures required a minute that there were 'nine dissenting'.

That last minute quoted reminds us that, although a good deal of the day-to-day managerial responsibility for Independent churches was in the hands of deacons and other officers, consultation and participation were, as we have seen, cherished Independent principles. A local church might record an 'order' to its elders that they write a letter expressing the congregation's views - and the Yarmouth church set down in writing how objections to proposals should be put to the elders. Independent records show that congregational democracy was a reality, though, as has been indicated, the quest was for unanimity or consensus rather than a majority. Even so, the Independent churches did not necessarily pursue the endless search for agreement that seems to have characterised Quaker procedures, and a form of majority rule can be seen in an example from the Norwich church book, in which a proposal was entered as having received general assent, with two dissidents recorded, 'notwithstanding' which, the church 'did proceed in the work ... And ... it was assented by the whole by the signe of Lifting up their hand except the two brethren before mentioned'.

**Church construction, re-building, church furniture and management of premises**

A considerable amount of material is available on the building and re-building of Independent meeting houses. Some of this information may come from historical sketches, initially mostly manuscript and sometimes printed in chapel or denominational histories. These are often highly authoritative, based on or made up of recollections by active participants in the building programmes of chapels:

> (Hindley, Lancs.):
> When the Nonconformists commenced their work of faith and labour of love in Hindley, many were the annoyances to which they were subjected. They first met together in a thatched-roof cottage near the Lord Nelson Inn, ... afterwards in a joiner's shop belonging to a Mr. Wm. Livsey,... and so mightily grew the word of God and prevailed that the band of Nonconformists saw the necessity of increased accommodation, and they removed to an upper room in the lower part of Market Street, where divine worship was conducted until the erection of St. Paul's Chapel.

The launching of the building venture referred to in the final phrase of the last extract was recorded in a financial appeal minuted by the congregation. These appeals were often published in explicitly catholic terms - for instance, one, at Wigan, 1817, was addressed to all 'who, with a liberality unbiassed by party or sectarian spirit, have ever been manifested a dispostition to promote any place or institution which may tend to the general benefit of society'.

> (Hindley, 1807)
> We, a few Protestant Dissenters of the Independent Denomination, in the township of Hindley, in the County of Lancaster, humbly beg the assistance of all well disposed persons of every description, for the purpose of building a chapel in the village of Hindley aforesaid,...

When the work went ahead (in this case after a few years' delay), its progress was monitored by the minuted reports of the Lancashire Congregational Union, a body produced by the late 18th and early 19th century northern Independent renaissance and by the trend towards associational structures in regional Independency quite late in the period of this survey. The Union had a brief of encouraging and overseeing 'the erection of new meeting houses', and its annual reports (in Lancashire Record Office) chart steady progress in the provision of chapel accommodation:

> (Standish, Lancs.,1815)
> Of late, another room has been taken for conducting the religious services, far more commodious, and more eligibly situated than the old place, which was remarkably damp and uncomfortable. In this new place there is a much better attendance than formerly; ... .

The Union's reports tend to be concerned with observing a net increase in chapel

buildings and the accompanying numerical provision of seating - though there
are certainly vivid structural details, like the sharply delineated word-picture of
a 'humble place of worship', the low-cost (£70) wood, clay, and straw chapel built
within a month at North Meols, Lancs. Individual church books may be more
informative on internal structural details, for instance, the structural history of
the simple ungalleried chapel at Wigan, which was initially (1818) 'five yards
high', but, in 1820, was elevated and given three galleries, the new work
amounting to almost double the cost of the first structure.

Now that Nonconformist church architecture is being taken more seriously as a
subject of study[10], chapel buildings may themselves recount their own structural histories, especially in the inscriptions (however laconic) that their visitors
can read or which their historians have recorded:

| (Wigan) | ST PAUL' | (St Helen's) | Old Chapel 1710 |
|---------|----------|--------------|-----------------|
|         | CHAPEL   |              | New Chapel 1826 |
|         | 1815     |              | Enlarged 1869   |
|         |          |              | Enlarged 1883   |

Church books of individual Independent congregations accord a certain amount
of space to the routine tasks of running and maintaining church premises. The
restrained opulence of a metropolitan congregation can be read into entries like
the resolution 'that a new and handsome Door Case be made to the entrance of
the passage from Fetter Lane'; the packed atmosphere of long and repeated
services in the East Anglian capital comes across vividly in a minuted instruction
to clear the meeting chamber after Sunday morning worship 'in order to the
Cooling' of the room 'in preparation for the afternoon session. Premises, their
upkeep, ownership and registration, were of course matters of the greatest importance, and vital documents, such as a 1710 deed of gift (by a deceased
minister) donating land for a meeting house, needed to be drawn up with exact
notarial punctilio, even specifying what should happen to the property should
toleration come to an end.

Independent church books cover a wide range of topics, from covenants and
professions of faith to the minutes of discipline and of building plans and
maintenance. Above all, these are church records which reveal the proceedings
and thinking of Independency's vital unit, the local congregation.

### Research material other than church minutes

For Independency's basic credal statement, *The Savoy Declaration of Faith and
Order*, see the edition, with a most valuable introduction, by A.G. Matthews
(London, 1959). For post-Restoration Independency's most influential minister,
see *The Correspondence of John Owen (1616-1683) With an account of his life
and work*, ed. Peter Toon (Cambridge and London, 1970). Alexander Gordon's
*Freedom After Ejection. A Review (1690-1692) of Presbyterian and Congrega-
tional Nonconformity in England and Wales* (London and Manchester, 1917) is
a fully edited version in print of a nationwide survey of congregations, their
ministers and financial circumstances in a period of Presbyterian-Independent
unity: see also, from that period the 'Heads of Agreement', 1691, in Williston

Walker, *The Creeds and Platforms of Congregationalism* (1893, reprinted Boston and Philadelphia, 1969), pp.455-462. For one of the best known (if liberal or even unorthodox) 18th-century Independents, see Philip Doddridge, *Ten Sermons on the Power and Grace of Christ, And on the Evidences of His Glorious Gospel* (various editions, e.g. the 4th edn., London 1760); J.D. Humphreys, ed., *The Correspondence and Diary of Philip Doddridge* (London, 1830); and Job Orton, *Memoirs of the Life, Character and Writings of the Late Reverend Philip Doddridge* (Shrewsbury, 1766). Malcolm Deacon has produced a readable account, with documentary material and appendices, *Philip Doddridge of Northampton, 1702-51* (Northampton, 1980). Manuscript letters of Philip Doddridge (*et al*) are in New College, London, with a microfilm in D.W.L. Also in D.W.L., the Correspondence of John Blackburn 1791-1855), minister and editor of the *Congregational Magazine*. Note also in New College, Edinburgh: the diary, sermons, etc. of the Hants. minister, David Bogue (1750-1825); in Lambeth Palace Library: the correspondence of William Bull (1738-1814), minister of Newport Pagnell; in the PRO Northern Ireland: the diary, 1812-15, of the London minister, William Johnson Fox (1786-1864); in the Northants. Record Office: the correspondence of the Northants. minister, Thomas Northcote Toller (1756-1821).

### Notes to Chapter 3

1.    R Tudur Jones, *Congregationalism in England, 1662-1962*, (London, 1962), Ch. 1-4; Watts *The Dissenters*, I, pp. 99-103, 130-3, 135-6, 152-9, 219, 268-270, 273, 289-298, 376-9, 467-9.

2.    From D.W.L.: Church Book of Fetter Lane Independent Chapel, pp. 6-9 (1782-3).

3.    In the elaborate documentation accompanying a 'call' to the ministry, attempts might be made to represent the consensus of a church over a candidate, perhaps through the composition of supporting letters from sections of the congregation, such as its youth. This could lead to some fairly unconvincing writing, as in the case of the Southwold Independent church whose 'Young People' in 1824 sent a letter to a prospective minister assuring him that they were 'highly gratified by the pleasing intelligence that the members of the Church have given you a call to the pastoral office'. (D.W.L.: Southwold, Suffolk, Independent Church Book, 1748-1850, p.40).

4.    D.W.L.: Great Yarmouth Church Book 1642-1813 (transcribed), p. 53 ff. (1675).

5.    *Ibid.*, p. 110. Indeed, inter-congregational activity and organisation were relatively strong in East Anglia: in 1667 the Norwich church called upon 'the churches' of the region for help with a particularly intractable disciplinary case: D.W.L.: The Church Book Belonging to a Society of Christians who assemble... at the Old Meeting Norwich, p.47.

6.   Yarmouth Church Book, pp. 146-7 (c.1686). It may be that Mr Frazor
     had been advocating something alien to traditional Independency, a
     fully developed synodical Scots Presbytery, which was far from the
     reality of English Presbyterianism after, and perhaps even before,
     1660. Co-operation between Presbyterians and Independents in East
     Anglia is evident, for example, in an invitation sent from the Yarmouth
     church for 'some pastors of the presbyterian persuasion' to attend an
     ordination (*ibid.*, p. 151, 1688).

7.   Jones, *Congregationalism*, pp. 80-1, 125-6.

8.   Fetter Lane Minutes, pp. 17-18 (1785); and compare the expulsion of
     a Norwich church member who had decided 'to walk no more with
     this Church but with the duch Congregation... '. (Norwich Minutes, p.
     47, 1667).

9.   D.W.L.: Wattisfield, Suffolk, Church Book, p. ff. (1679).

10.  See in particular the Royal Commission on the Historical Monuments
     of England, *An Inventory of Nonconformist Chapels and Meeting
     Houses in Central England*, (London, 1986) which covers 13 counties
     and all the denominations, contains detailed chapel histories and is
     lavishly illustrated with photographs and elevations.

**Sources for Chapter 3**

Excerpts from manuscript material in this chapter come from Independent
church minute books in D.W.L.: Wattisfield, Suffolk, Church Book; Southwold,
Suffolk, Independent Church Book, 1748-1850; Great Yarmouth Church Book
1642-1913 (transcribed); Church Book of [London] Fetter Lane Independent
Chapel; The Church Book belonging to a Society of Christians who assemble ...
at the Old Meeting Norwich.

See also B. Nightingale, *Lancashire Nonconformity; or Sketches, Historical &
Descriptive, of the Congregational and Old Presbyterian Church in the County*
(6 unnumbered volumes, Manchester, n.d. [1890-3]; W. Gordon Robinson, *A
History of the Lancashire Congregational Union 1806-1956* (Manchester, 1955).
H.G. Tibbutt has produced two helpful guides: 'Congregational Church Records',
*Archives*, v (1961), p. 7, and 'Sources for Congregational church history',
*Transactions of the Congregational History Soc.*, xix (1960).

Some selected repositories for Independent archives include the following:

Essex: Essex Record Office, Chelmsford: Coggeshall Independents' Minutes,
1775-1897 (3 vols), with Accounts (mostly for church building), 1687-1834 (4
vols.), plus deeds, 1707-1882, and Sunday and day school minutes and accounts,
1788-1883 (9 vols); Stanstead, Mountfitchet Old and New Meetings, Minutes and
Registers of Baptisms and Burials, 1822-84 (4 vols.) and including historical

accounts of these churches, 1698-1865 with names of members, 1776-1882, and a plan and elevation of about 1780; Witham Independents' Record Book and Minutes, 1845-1928 (8 vols.), including the names of members and register of baptisms, marriages and burials, with accounts, 1715-1935 (9 vols.); Romford Independents' Church Book, 1779-1857, with Register of Baptisms and Burials, 1779-1854.

Dorset: P.R.O.: Charmouth Independents' Baptisms, 1780; Lyme Regis Independents' Baptisms, 1775.

Somerset: P.R.O.: Chard Independents' Baptisms, 1786; Pitminster Independents' Baptisms, 1709; Wellington Independent Baptisms, 1786.

Cornwall:  Cornwall Record Office, Truro: Creed Independent Chapel, Lists of Members, 1820-1921; P.R.O.: St Austell Independents' Baptisms, 1789-1835; Fowey Mount Zion Chapel Baptisms, 1798-1836; Lostwithiel Independent Chapel, Baptisms, 1812-1837; Truro Independents' Baptisms, 1769-1837.

Devon: Devon Record Office, Exeter: Kingsbridge Independents' (formerly Presbyterians) Burials, 1793; P.R.O.: Buckfastleigh Independents' Baptisms, 1787-1837; Chudleigh Independents' (formerly Presbyterians) Baptisms, 1711-1837; Exeter Castle Lane Meeting Baptisms, 1798-1836, and Burials, 1800-1836; Kingsbridge Independents' (formerly Presbyterians) Baptisms, 1775-1837; Ottery St. Mary's Independents' (formerly Presbyterians) Baptisms, 1746-1837.

# CHAPTER IV

## RECORDS OF THE METHODIST CHURCH

### Introduction

In contrast with Independency, which generally did not develop complex federal or nationwide structures during our period, Methodism evolved elaborate networks of church government. Like Methodism's parent, the Church of England, or for that matter like the Society of Friends, the Methodist churches have traditionally had arrangements for linking the individual 'societies' to an area superstructure which leads up to a regional apparatus and then to a national body. A characteristic Methodist organisational model is that of societies grouped in local circuits, these being associated into area districts, with the conference as the national forum. Like the broadly similar structures of the Society of Friends, this pyramid arrangement was essentially practical and administrative and could be adapted freely to meet altered circumstances.

This chapter, will consider some of Methodism's sub-divisions, which arose as a result of disagreements over church order and discipline and over such questions as the relative roles of ministry and laity in the church. The survey will begin by looking at some archival sources for a form of Methodism - a Calvinistic variant - which is chronologically senior to the non-Calvinistic form associated with the Wesleys. It will then consider records of administrative bodies within Wesleyan Methodism, from the national conference down to the individual society or 'chapel'. Finally, there will be investigation of some sources for the history of splinter groups from Wesleyan Methodism.

Methodism arose in the 1730s as part of a widespread aspiration, throughout Britain, the rest of Europe and in Britain's American colonies, towards a religion of the feelings in the midst of the rationalist Enlightenment. The Gloucester-born George Whitefield (1714-1770) underwent a 'new birth' of religious conversion at Oxford early in 1735. The brothers John (1703-1791) and Charles (1707-1788) Wesley, Anglican clergymen from a clerical family, both experienced religious conversions in 1738 which were directly linked to the re-discovery of an essential Reformation principle, justification by faith. The elder brother, John, was an organising genius, a tireless missionary, and essentially Anglican in his conception of a mission to the people of England at large. Until his death in 1791, John Wesley struggled to avoid a secession from the Church of England, a split which seems to us today, with hindsight at least, to have been largely unavoidable. Before considering the further development of 'Wesleyan' Methodism and its records, we may review the evolution of Methodism's first important sub-division and some of its documentary sources.

### Calvinistic Methodism

The Wesleys' senior in the Oxford 'Holy Club' in the 1730s was George Whitefield. In common with the Welsh revivalist, Howell Harris (1714-177), George Whitefield was attracted to the bedrock Calvinist theology of English Protestantism, though he did not share the organising talent that made Harris the founder of a cohesively structured Calvinistic Methodism in Wales.[1] Even so

Calvinistic Methodism became an important movement in England, though eventually over-shadowed by John Wesley's 'Arminian' variant. We shall be considering English Calvinistic Methodism's archives with reference to the two main sub-divisons of the movement, George Whitefield's followers and the 'Connexion' of the Countess of Huntingdon (1707-1791)). To do so, we shall briefly consider minutes of the Calvinistic Methodists' National Association as well as minutes of a leading London chapel of Whitefield's persuasion, the London Tabernacle, and those of a congregation within the Countess of Huntingdon's Connexion, the London Spa Fields Chapel.

John Wesley's public repudiation in 1740 of Calvinist positions on predestination alienated George Whitefield and in 1741 he 'separated from Mr. Wesley on their difference about election ...'. Although attempts continued to maintain a degree of harmony between these two major theological wings of Methodism, the establishment of the London Tabernacle in the early 1740s as the leading unit in the Calvinistic movement and the later creation of an English Calvinistic Methodist Association gave institutional expression to doctrinal disharmony.

**The Calvinistic Methodist Association**
The early minutes of this body, from 1745-9, are incorporated in the minute book of the London Tabernacle (see below), which in turn forms part of the archives of the Presbyterian Church of Wales kept in the Trevecka MS (2946) in the National Library of Wales, Aberystwyth. The quarterly Association brought together 'the societies in Connexion together under the care of the Reverend Mr Whitefield', the individual 'societies' being arranged by area: three (or five) in London, three in Gloucestershire, three in the Bristol-Bath area, five in the far west and others in the Midlands. By 1747, 29 Calvinist Methodist societies were being brought together in their Association, meeting alternately in London, Bristol, Wiltshire and Gloucestershire. Much of the Association's time was taken up resolving theological questions; for example, meeting at Bristol in March 1745, the members present agreed on the scripturality of infant baptism and an ordained ministry, and issued statements of Reformation doctrine: '... Christ alone is our compleat righteousness, holiness and sanctification', a theme elaborately pursued. Here then, the minuted proceedings of meetings were establishing the doctrinal consensus of an emergent church, and in doing so, they point unmistakably to difficult, protracted sessions attended by individuals with firm views and sensitive consciences. However, after the drama of a major departure to the Moravians, these minutes of the Calvinistic Methodist federal Association tend, as it were, to settle down, and to deal with the rather more humdrum matters of the allocation of preachers, the review of ministrial candidates, cash acounts and the acquisition of a 'playhouse' for preaching.[2]

**The Calvinistic Methodist Society**
Records of individual societies within English Calvinistic Methodism can be sub-divided into those of the Countess of Huntingdon's Connexion and those of Whitefield's followers. Available in print, edited by C. E. Welch, are the minutes, from 1778 to 1811, of the Spa Fields Chapel of the Countess of Huntingdon's Connexion, the original being lodged in Cheshunt College, Cambridge, along with the chapel account book (1794-6), chapel school

accounts (1782-1807) and charity accounts (1780-6); the chapel's register of baptisms (1783-1837) and of burials (1778-1849) are in the P.R.O. Records of other individual societies of the Connexion are, apparently, rare, at least for our period. On the other hand, some thousands of letters and papers associated with the Countess and her religious work are to be found in Cheshunt College, covering the period from about 1768. Other surviving papers of the Countess are in the Huntington Library, California, and in Leicester City Museum. Also in print, edited by Dr Welch, are the minutes, 1743-7, of the London Tabernacle of George Whitefield's Connexion, the original being amongst the Trevecka MSS. in the National Library of Wales, Aberystwyth. Some Whitefieldian societies, for example in Gloucestershire, Plymouth and London, assumed a Congrega-tionalist identity and their records, which are not plentiful, became those of the Congregational churches into which they evolved. Government in the individual Calvinistic Methodist societies varied in its character from the relative democ-racy of the Whitefieldian groups to the close patronal control exercised by the Countess of Huntingdon in the societies of her sub-division of Calvinistic revivalism. In the societies that came under George Whitefield's leadership, once a month a 'general conference' of the whole society met 'to confer on all affairs of the whole Society and settle all matters relating thereto...'. However, the community also had a steering committee meeting weekly and consisting of the 'visitors of classes and bands', along with the 'resident ministers', jointly discussing matters of a general nature only, usually without separate minutes. Women's governmental role was severely restricted.

In contrast to the relatively high levels of congregational self-government in Whitefield's societies, the Countess of Huntingdon retained close personal supervision of the government of her Connexion and, at her patronal chapel at Spa Fields, London, the twelve-man management committee set up by the Countess regularly sent progress reports and accounts to her and referred changes in the composition of the committee to her: 'Agreed, with Lady Huntingdon's permission' is a characteristic entry in minutes.

Some differences in recorded business between these two variants of Georgian Calvinistic revivalism may be accounted for as much as anything by chronology and geography, especially social geography. To take the example of church charity, in the proceedings of the Shoreditch-based Calvinistic Methodists of George Whitefield's connection, this matter is approached as an interchange between church members, most of whom shared a degree of poverty or near poverty. At the more opulent Spa Fields community of the Countess's Connex-ion on the other hand, charity was a function distinguishing the average church member from a clearly demarcated group of 'the poor who attend the worship of God in this chapel...'.

Alongside some exacting moral discipline, doctrine and its niceties loom large in the minutes at the Tabernacle: 'Mr. Cudworth's ... introducing antinomianism ... and Brother Cennick's drinking into the Moravian spirit'. It has to be said that in that formative period, especially the 1740s, of the Evangelical Revival new churches were beginning to form out of a magma of conflicting theologies and needed to solidify their doctrinal positions. In contrast, later in the century, with theological viewpoints somewhat more established, the Countess's Connexion, at least in its London headquarters, was more likely to be pre-occupied with defining its relationship, an embattled one of legal disputation, with the Church of England.

A notable difference in items recorded between the minutes of the Whitefieldian Tabernacle and those of the Countess's Spa Fields Chapel is the absence of practical concerns in the minutes of the former, some matters of that nature, such as the lease of premises, being dealt with by the Association. Both chapels were existing buildings before their minuted records began, Whitefield noting in 1741, 'my friends are erecting a place, which I have called a *Tabernacle*, for morning exposition'. Items concerning the premises are not a significant feature of the Tabernacle minutes, though in the case of the Spa Fields Chapel, a pre-existent building converted from secular use, alterations and additions took up some space in the minutes:

> Mr Carr laid before us two plans for a vestry, one within the chapel, the other without. The latter was adopted after considering the conveniences and inconveniences of both: chiefly because the great stairs must have been taken away to make the vestry within the chapel, which are of much use, both as affording room to many poor persons to stand or sit on, and also for people to come down out of the gallery when service is ended. Mr Carr was of opinion it might be done for about 60 guineas.

Such basic practicality - 'Mr James Nokes ... signed a contract to build the intended vestry, together with a privy, for seventy pounds...' - could, even so, be combined with more elevated matters, as when the Spa Fields clerk recorded, in great detail, an ordination, with an account of the 'christian experience' of the ordinand.

**Wesleyan Methodism**

For some years before the final departure of Lady Huntingdon's Calvinistic Methodists from the Church of England and their emergence effectively as a new Nonconformist denomination, the emphatically non-Calvinistic Methodism of the Wesley brothers had been making steady strides in terms of mass evangelisation and the evolution of its own structures: indeed, highly articulate organisation was a hallmark of these men, or at least of John Wesley, whose cult of efficiency had earned them the nickname 'Methodists' at Oxford. The structure as it evolved was pyramidical, with the particular 'society' at its base. This was itself divided up into 'bands' for the religiously more advanced members (perhaps four in each band), and 'classes' of up to twelve in each class and making up the society's whole membership. These fellowships met weekly under band or class leaders.

John Wesley grouped the local societies into circuits, whose representatives (from 1748) met quarterly, each circuit issuing a 'plan' locating preachers between the societies. Ceaselessly active and, it has to be said, markedly autocratic, Wesley retained overall control of the societies throughout his lifetime and enjoyed, even posthumously, enormous prestige and authority.

However, deputies acting for Wesley - 'assistants', later to be known as 'super-intendents' - were placed in the circuits.

Since the Methodist organisation first arose simply as a convenient, efficient associational structure with no pretensions of ecclesiastical status, it could readily adapt to changing circumstances: for example, the areas of circuits shrank as the numbers of societies within them increased with the growth of Wesley's movement. A further adaptation following the early creation of the circuits was the estabishment of districts grouping circuits together. Then, in 1744, Wesley himself brought together a ten-man conference to advance the movement's organisation, establish its mainstream Protestant doctrines and, in the long run vainly, head off any secessionist potential it might have to abandon the established Church.

## The Conference

Available in printed form, the national conference minutes record the ample deliberations of Methodism's most senior body - an institution whose proceed-ings and format of business obviously influenced the various areas bodies throughout the country. In the period 1765-1798, conference met by alternation in Manchester, Leeds, London and Bristol. A question-and-answer arrangement was adopted for the recorded proceedings and the sessions were much taken up with overseeing the preaching ministry: what preachers were on probation; who had given up itinerant preaching; the identities of assistants; possible objections to any preachers; the distribution of preachers by area; and, rather colourfully, what was being done to ensure that preachers did not combine their religious work with hawking 'pills, drops, balsams, or medicines of any kind'. The conference also reviewed the numerical strength of the movement area by area, looked at its financial health, considered opportunities in Scotland and Ireland, made arrangements for morning and evening preaching, and so on. As we shall see, breakway groups from Wesleyan Methodism also formed national confer-ences, with similar schedules of agenda.

## The District

Sometimes compared with an Anglican diocese, the Wesleyan Methodist district stood at a mid-point of the chain of authority between the national conference and the local circuit. The business of the meetings was recorded in the same interrogative form adopted by the conference:

> Qu. 1 - Are there any objections against any of the Preachers of this District? Answr: -- None

Agenda items include: consideration of 'Deficiencies', i.e. shortfalls, in the accounts of the preachers' expenses; names of probationary preachers; nomi-nees to the conference; building proposals; possible objections to preachers; the recommendation of preachers to the conference; any candidates for itinerant ministry and the foreign missions. The minutes, naturally, became fuller as business expanded with the growth of the denomination, so that by the early 19th century the minutes were dealing with such matters as: preachers' obedience to the church's rules and giving good example; complaints against any of the preaching brethren; admissions to 'full Connection'; reviews of probationary preachers; collections for chapels and new buildings; financial accounts; consideration of boy pupils for the school John Wesley had founded at Kingswood; girls' educational allowances; representatives to the 'Stationing Committee'; dress regulations for preachers; and the recording of preachers' deaths, with obituary notices. The minutes of districts also help us chart the rapid growth of Wesleyan Methodism, which increased in numbers from 72,000 in 1791 to almost 200,000 in 1820: new chapels were recorded and rules set out for building them, circuits were sub-divided and new circuits created and the undoubted financial strain of providing a preaching ministry is unmistakeably conveyed.

District minutes also accorded considerable space to doctrinal reviews, the maintenance of Wesleyan orthodoxy and the avoidance of 'error in Doctrine', by sticking close to the founder, his sermons and writings. With their insistence in holding a firm doctrinal line, they provide a vantage point from which to watch the disputes that rent the Methodist movement after the death of John Wesley:

> Do we all believe & teach the old Methodist Doctrines, Vizt: Original Sin, The Divinity of our Lord Jesus Christ, Justification by faith, the direct witness of the Spirit, Christian Perfection, & the eternity of the Torments of Hell, in the proper Methodist sense of those Doctrines?

At the same time, district minutes may combine considerable theological rigour - 'we judge this article to be antimethodistical ... Calvinistic sentiments' - with a good deal of routine practical business: the 'defective' deeds of the Banbury and Buckingham chapels, for instance, which did not allow their trustees to mortgage them as necessary; along with precisely tabulated collections and detailed preachers' expenses down to items like £5-6-6d for 'Coals & Candles'.

The Methodist districts were part of a nationwide network and therefore stereotyping of the form of their records was not only inevitable but, from the point of view of the emergent Methodist church, entirely desirable. Thus, whereas in many of the Nonconformist archives we have been considering in other chapters there is heterogeneity in the forms assumed by records of congregations, in two pre-eminently federal bodies each characterised by a hierarchy of delegate assemblies, the Society of Friends and the Wesleyan Methodists, we can see the emergence both of common formats for recording proceedings and also a repetition of transactions between one area body and another. Nevertheless, despite standardisation, district minutes also show up some local and regional variations and emphases, especially in reporting the deaths of beloved local preachers:

> John Braithwaite ... was a Native of Parton ... his Parents were respected members of the Church of England and designed him for the Ministry of the Church, he was ... providentially ... brought to the knowledge of the truth, joined the Society, and soon began to act as a Local Preacher among us, ... He was a Man of good natural abilities, deep piety, amiable temper, and extensive usefulnes ...

## The Circuit

In the history of the organisational evolution of Methodism, the circuit precedes the district as an area body. The circuit handled a good deal of routine business, much of it financial. Circuit records, which have been and are being placed in considerable numbers in local and county record offices, deal with finance and administration. A typical example is the 'Circuit Book' of the Colne Wesleyan Methodist circuit in East Lancashire which itemises contributions from the thirteen individual societies within that circuit (£10 from Colne itself, over £31 in all), and disbursements, mostly for ministerial expenses: 'One child', 'Washing', 'Letters', 'Carriage of Boxes', 'Coals'. Individual donations, often quite generous, were made to meet expenses. The arrangement and presentation are orderly and exact:

| Disbursements [1815] | |
| --- | --- |
| Mr Midgleys Quarterage ... | 4  4 0 |
| One child ... | 1 11 6 |
| Board  ... | 9  2 0 |
| Washing and Letters ... | 1 12 0 |
| Coals and Candles for six months ... | 3 18 3 |
| House Bill ... | 1  4 3 |
| Doctors Bill ... | 15 0 |
| Mr Worralls Quarterage ... | 4  4 0 |
| Mrs W... Do. ... | 4  4 0 |

The circuit and its records were also the appropriate place for recording items of registry, including lists of births and baptisms which could conveniently be entered in tabular form: for example:

| Children and Parents Names | Township | Parish | When Born | When Baptized | By whom Baptized |
| --- | --- | --- | --- | --- | --- |
| Joseph Ainsworth son of Timothy & Sally Ainsworth | Over Darwen | Blackburn | September 22nd 1794 | Novr 2 1794 | Thomas Taylor |

Perhaps the most important function of the circuit was the preparation of the 'circuit plans' which begin in 1777, exist in great profusion, and are entirely typical of the systematic Methodist way of doing things. Two examples are given overleaf.

Since the sermon was the mainstay of Methodist worship, the emergent denomination devised the circuit plan as a method of distributing preachers around the circuit area, thereby providing a current of reasonably fresh preaching and also, it was hoped, preventing any preacher's building up a devoted local following which might result in secession. Initially, the circuit plans, separate documents giving about 1000 different schedules for preachers before 1860, were written out, but later printed. In the timing of Sunday services, every attempt was made to avoid clashes with parish worship: thus, in the 1811 Burnley circuit plan, the timing of a service at 9 a.m. in Burnley and Padiham makes way for the Church service, whereas in Accrington, without a church, the Methodist sevice occupied the 'prime time' of 10.30.

The 1786 Colne circuit plan, reproduced from a local Methodist church history, provides an example of the punishing 'six weeks' round', meaning that the preacher for whom the plan was a schedule completed his tour over six weeks. There were three preachers in this circuit, so that, for example, the first preacher would be at Colne on the first Sunday, the second preacher on the second Sunday and the third preacher on the third Sunday, and so on, around the circuit. The Colne plan gives the clearest impression of the ferocious demands of Sunday and weekday preaching, literally morning, noon and night, over a round of 230 miles.

## A PLAN FOR PREACHING IN THE COLNE CIRCUIT IN THE YEAR 1786

| DAYS | PLACE | TIMES | SERVICES | MILES | DAYS | PLACE | TIMES | SERVICES | MILES |
|---|---|---|---|---|---|---|---|---|---|
| 1st Sunday | Colne | Morning | | | 4th Sunday | Bolton Hall | Morning | | |
| " | Do. | noon } | 3 | 0 | " | Blackburn | noon } | 3 | 5 |
| " | Do. | night | | | " | Do. | night | | |
| Monday | Stocks | | 1 | 6 | Monday | Ribchester | | 1 | 6 |
| Tuesday | Caxton | Noon } | 2 | 10 | Tuesday | Blackburn | | 1 | 6 |
| " | Mawen | night | | | | | | | |
| Wednesday | Long Preston | Noon } | 2 | 10 | Wednesday | Grave | noon } | 2 | 8 |
| " | Settle | night | 2 | 13 | " | Flaxmoss | night | | |
| Thursday | Wigglesworth-row | Noon } | 2 | 8 | Thursday | Bank-Top | noon | 2 | 5 |
| " | Newhurst | night | | | " | Mill-end | | | |
| Friday | Gisburn | Noon } | | | Friday | Syke-side | | | |
| " | Rimmingham | night | 2 | 7 | | | | | |
| Saturday | Padiham all day and rest | | | 10 | Saturday | Haslingden | | | |
| 2nd Sunday | Padiham | Morning | | | 5th Sunday | Do. | Morning | | |
| " | Do. | noon } | 3 | 0 | " | Mill-end | noon } | 3 | 7 |
| " | Do. | night | | | " | Bacup | night | | |
| Monday | Do. | | 1 | | Monday | Do. | | 1 | 0 |
| Tuesday | Burnley | | 1 | 3 | Tuesday | Wardleford | | 1 | 8 |
| Wednesday | Rough-Lea | | 1 | 6 | Wednesday | Longclough Top | Noon } | 2 | 8 |
| Thursday | Colne | | 1 | 4 | " | Todmorden | night | | |
| Friday | Haggat | | 1 | 3 | Thursday | Rothwell-end | | 1 | 2 |
| Saturday | Rothwell-end | | 1 | 14 | Friday | Luddington | | 1 | 6 |
| 3rd Sunday | Todmorden | Morning | | | Saturday | Stocks | | 1 | 2 |
| " | Do. | noon } | 3 | 2 | 6 th Sunday | Do. | Morning | | |
| " | Do. | night | | | " | Heptonstall | noon } | 3 | 2 |
| Monday | Top o'th' Close | | 1 | 14 | " | Do. | night | | |
| Tuesday | Harwood | Noon } | 2 | 9 | Monday | Do. | | 1 | 0 |
| " | Blackburn | night | | | Tuesday | Widdup | noon } | | |
| Wednesday | Preston | | 1 | 12 | " | Southfield | night | 2 | 10 |
| Thursday | Do. | | 1 | 0 | Wednesday | Fowlrigg | | 1 | 4 |
| Friday | Chorley | | 1 | 10 | Thursday | Colne | | 1 | 2 |
| Saturday | Bolton Hall | | 1 | 10 | Friday | Barrowford | | 1 | 2 |
| | | | | | Saturday | Colne | | 2 | |

The circuit plan for the Burnley area in 1811, reproduced from a local Methodist church history, was accompanied by a list of the itinerant preachers, twenty-seven of them in that circuit. The plan is now in the form of a diary for a half year period. Service times, M for morning, A for afternoon and E for evening, are given, and the timetable indicates that in some populous places such as Burnley, there were three Sunday services (1½ = 1.30 p.m.) and in others perhaps only an afternoon service or only an evening one. According to the plan, preacher number 2 on the accompanying listed key would be in Burnley for the three sessions on 5 May, whereas preacher number 1 would be in Padiham, there to be followed on the 12th of the month by preacher number 5, and so on.

## PLAN OF BURNLEY CIRCUIT, 1811.

| PLACES | TIME (M A E) | MAY 5 12 19 26 | JUNE 2 9 16 23 30 | JULY 7 14 21 28 | AUGUST 4 11 18 25 | SEPT 1 8 15 22 29 | OCT 6 13 20 27 | N 3 |
|---|---|---|---|---|---|---|---|---|
| Burnley | Morning 9 | 2 1 1 1 | 1 1 2 2 2 | 1 1 2 1 | 1 2 2 2 | 1 1 2 1 1 | 2 2 2 1 | 1 |
| Burnley | Afternoon 1 | 2 1L 2 7 | 1 1 2 3 2 | 1S 2 5 1 | 1 2L 7 2 | 1 2 13 1 1S | 2 14 2 1 | 1L |
| Burnley | Evening 6 | 2 1 2 7 | 1 1 2 3 2 | 1 2 5 1 | 1 2 7 2 | 1 2 13 1 1 | 2 14 2 1 | 1 |
| Padiham | Morning 9 | 1 2 | 2 1 1 | 2 2 | 1 1 | 2 2 | 1 1 | 2 |
| Padiham | Afternoon 1½ | 1 5 1 2 | 2 11 1 2 1 | 7 1L 2 2 | 4 1 2 1 | 7 12 2L 16 | 1 2 1 5 | 2 |
| Padiham | Evening 7 | 1 5 1 2 | 2 11 1 2 1 | 7 1 2 2 | 4 1 2 1 | 7 1 2 2 3 | 1 2 1 5 | 2 |
| Accrington | Morning 10½ | 24 2 21 1 | 26 27 1 20 | 2 5 1 22 | 2 7 1 23 | 2 6 1 20 2 | 18 1 5 2 | 17 |
| Accrington | Afternoon 1 | 24 2 21 1 | 26 27 1 20 | 2L 5 1S 22 | 2 7 1 23 | 2 6 1 20 2 | 18 1L5 2 | 17 |
| Accrington | Evening 7 | 2 1 | 2 1 | 2 1 | 2 1 | 2 1 2 | 1 2 | |
| Oakenshaw | 6 | 11 P | 6 P 7 | P 8 | P 11 | P 6 | P 7 | P |
| Warren Lane | 6 | 23 11 | 18 6 25 | 7 18 | 8 27 | 22 11 | 7 27 | 6 |
| Whalley | 1 6 | 18 3 | 17 6 | 9 19 | 10 21 | 11 7 19 | 6 11 | |
| Higham | 4 | 3 9 | 10 12 | 4 3 | 5 11 | 12 3 9 | 10 4 | |
| Mereclough | 1 | 5 13 | 4 9 12 | 10 5 | 11 3 | 9 12 | 10 4 | 5 |
| Lowerhouse | 3 | 12 10 | 3 9 | 11 4 | 3 5 | 10 9 11 | 3 10 | |
| New Laund | 6 | 9 | 4 | 3 | 12 | 9 | 10 | 4 |

### The Individual Society

Below the circuit, the nucleus of organised Methodist life was the individual society or chapel, their recorded proceedings containing a certain emphasis on management, finance and building development. A major financial resource, carefully listed were the 'pew rents'. Rents on a monthly or quarterly basis were recorded by name with perhaps pew numbers, and group payments, obviously for families. Sums collected under this head could be substantial - at Colne over £16 in the first quarter of 1797 and over £24 in the course of the year. These business and financial documents from individual Methodist societies yield extensive information about the physical provisions, membership, trusteeship and building programmes in a period of rapid Methodist expansion. In many cases, minute books are in effect those of buildings sub-committees and can take us deep into details of planning and construction: the siting of buildings, their dimensions, the inspection of plans, the specification of materials for the fabric, the internal arrangements and galleries, subsidiary buildings (houses, school-rooms), correspondence with architects, and so on. Formal arrangements with builders, including   pricings, might be recorded separately, on loose leaves.[4]

Some light can be shed on Methodist building development by ministers' note-books, like those of the Yorkshire Dales minister, Jacob Rowell, and by church records such as the Dales Wesleyan Methodist circuit book, both deposited in Durham County Record Office. From such material, we can assemble a pattern of the growth of Methodism mirrored in its building programme in areas where it readily took root: for instance, the 1760 petition to Conference, granted in 1769, of Yorkshire's Swaledale Methodists for a chapel, which did duty until 1841, or the record of the chapel in Gunnerside built in 1789 for £600 on a piece of land bought from a Quaker.[5] Finance, though, was the over-riding considera-tion, as the records show. Indeed, a dominant concern with practicality, simplicity, economy and the ratio between modest cost and ample size, consis-tent (or not) with safety, may have meant that attention to architectural planning and aesthetics *as such* is not uppermost. Plans seem to have been intended primarily for tradesmen to consult: a Bacup, Methodist handbill advertising the construction of a new chapel in 1786 drew attention to the existence of plans 'for the inspection of Artificers and others'.[6] The classic statement of 19th-century Methodist architectural thinking, F. J. Jobson's *Chapel & School Architecture as appropriate to the buildings of nonconformists, particularly those of the Wesleyan Methodists*, came out in 1850, well beyond the end of the period of this survey. In the age of rapid Methodist growth, sources in the Methodist Archives at the John Rylands Library, Manchester, seem to suggest that the movement was, if anything, somewhat embarrassed by the high building costs consequent on its own expansion. According to a  letter of William Myles, dated 1814, 'he [John Wesley] would not let a Chapel be built unless two thirds of the money was subscribed before a stone was laid ..' and Joseph Entwistle recalled in 1837  that 'even in London they are embarrassed by the debts & rents of chapels recently built or rented ...'. [7] Though ample size was a major desideratum in chapel building, rapid numerical growth and Methodism's somewhat plebeian social profile were factors ensuring that few edifices came up to the superb standards of the Georgian mother church of London Wesleyan Methodism, the 'New Foundery' chapel of 1778.

The day-to-day maintenance of chapels once built is a prominent feature of Methodist minute books. Since record books of individual societies were working documents for clerks and the administrators of chapels, trustees and stewards, they may include rough jottings and *aides mémoires* for the clerks and treasurers: 1s-8d 'for Extra worke', 1s-6d 'for Cleaning Galleries', 5s-6d.' 'for Cleaning Preaching house', and so on. Again, as working books they were used as convenient places for storing loose papers of a contractual nature which needed to be conserved and, if necessary, consulted. Examples range from a formal, signed, attested agreement with a builder, to a hasty note minuting orders given to a cleaner who 'agrees to keep the Chapel and Vestry very clean and in good order ... he will scour the Pulpit stairs and keep them clean Gallery stairs the Chapel to be clean every Tuesday ... Also to conduct himself with propriety the tools used in makeing the Graves &c. to be taken in every day and not to be left out of doors as has been the case formerly'.

Records of individual Methodist societies tend to be largely concerned with the management, financing and physical accommodation of these societies. The classes which, as we saw, made up the societies might make their appearance through the vital cash contributions they made to society finance. The familiar enclosures record the indispensable administrative support work for worshipping communities: the bills for builders' labourer (2/- a day in early 19th century Lancashire); for materials from turpentine to nails; for the hire of horse and cart; for '23½ Quarts Ale' (7s 10d); and, rather more edifyingly, for Sunday school hymn books and bibles. A hard pressed steward who was making endless payments 'for Oil & Candles' and 'for the Preachers Horse' might draw the line at an expenses claim 'of about One pound and 2 pence for the Preachers Board' and send it back un-met.

None of this is to say that records of individual societies are devoid of any but practical interest. Society books might record major events such as chapel openings with considerable enthusiasm, and accounts of conversions were kept. Further illumination of the religious life of individual societies is amply available in such sources as entries from the extensive correspondence and memoirs of Methodists, though not all personal recollections can be guaranteed to have quite the same drama as this one:

> We had [at Colne in 1777] with much difficulty raised a fine large chapel: and being completed Mr. Wesley came to open it. Being much crowded ... and the timber of the galleries sufficiently strong, just when Mr. Wesley and I had got into the pulpit, before he began, all of a sudden one of the galleries sunk down, and abundance of people had legs, arms, or thighs broken ... the cries of such as were mained, and such as were frightened, were truly piercing ...

At Colne, they learned how to treat with builders and record the agreements.

## Methodist variants

Perhaps it is true that the combination in Methodism of doctrinal sensitivity and an integrated organisation made the Methodist churches somewhat prone to schism: a looser organisation, as with Independent congregations, might have allowed individual groups to pursue theological preferences; a less intense concern with theological definition, as with the Quakers, might have permitted a single national federation to hold together more successfully. In fact, one major separation in Methodism had features which put us somewhat in mind of Independency. The fiery evangelist, Alexander Kilham (1762-1798), was one of those Methodists anxious in the 1790s to sever Methodism's remaining links with the parent Church of England, to recognise that Methodist ministers could validly celebrate sacraments and to accept lay representation in Conference. In 1797 Kilham and a group of sympathisers left the Wesleyan main line to form an important branch of Methodism, the lay-orientated New Connexion, with about 5,000 adherents.

For all Kilham's insistence on the value of the individual society and its trustees, the New Connexion immediately evolved a Wesleyan-style national conference. From 1797 this body met annually in some of the great Northern and Midland industrial centres where New Connexion Methodism had so much of its strength: Newcastle-on-Tyne, Sheffield, Leeds and Hull, Liverpool and Manchester, Hanley and Nottingham. Minutes of this conference, available in the Methodist Archives Centre in the John Rylands Library of the University of Manchester, show the vast range of its business, and the trend in Kilham's New Connexion towards an authentically Methodist sysem of oversight of the societies by superior bodies. Proceedings included: surveys of probationary preachers, of retired itinerants and deceased preachers; objections to preachers and certification of preachers' moral and ministerial qualifications; the circulation of books and magazines to the circuits; the submission of preachers' financial accounts; annual collections; preachers' travel plans; attempts to get delegates to stay for the duration of the conference; identification of new chapels; rules revision and minuted correspondence, such as that with the disaffected Methodists of Lisburn, Co. Antrim, who were seeking to join the New Connexion.

As with the Wesleyan Methodist national conference, the business of the New Connexion conference expanded inexorably and its minuted record grew to an imposing twenty pages of manuscript in 1820, topics including: lists of members, including new members, of the conference; reviews of the 'state of the Connexion' town by town, including numbers of members (for example, 724 in Ashton but only 34 in London); a vast series of collections for various funds; and 'Private' resolutions not subsequently printed and other 'Private Minutes' subsequently printed.

It might be thought repetitious to consider all the sub-divisions of Methodism within the period of our survey: the Independent Methodists (first annual meeting, 1806 and strong in the North-West), the Methodist-influenced Bible Christians (1815), the Leeds-based Protestant Methodists (1827), and so on. Minutes of Conference of all the branches of Methodism are housed in the Methodist Archives Centre at Manchester. We shall also have the opportunity in our final chapter to consider sources for an outcrop of the Evangelical Revival, the Inghamites. To conclude our survey of Methodists materials, we might touch on those of just one other 'dissident' form of Methodism.

**Primitive Methodism**
Primitive Methodism, with its centre in the mining and pottery-working districts of North Staffordshire, was grouped around two leaders, the able organiser and preacher Hugh Bourne (1772-1852), and the fervent revivalist, William Clowes (1780-1851). Influenced by American experiments in *al fresco* revivalist 'camp meetings', Bourne took the lead in setting up such a gathering in the dramatic setting of Mow Cop, near Biddulph in North Staffordshire in May 1807. In the anti-revolutionary atmosphere of early 19th-century England, such meetings were open to suspicion of sedition and the national Methodist conference precipitately banned the assemblies. Between 1807 and 1810 Bourne, Clowes and their followers founded the Society of Primitive Methodists. The movement

recruited extensively from Staffordshire miners and pottery workers, East Anglian farm labourers and East Coast fishermen, ultimately making a major contribution to the rise of the labour movement.

In characteristic Methodist fashion, the Primitives quickly established a national conference, and its annual minutes in the Methodist Archives at Manchester, down to the re-amalgamation of the Primitives with other Methodists in 1932, form a superb historical source. The pattern of business and the interrogative form of the minutes, also used by the New Connexion, follow familiar Methodist patterns, with some variations: numerical reviews of the 'state of the Connexion' (in 1820 eight circuits and 7842 members); age limits for travelling preachers (45); scrutiny of ministerial candidates including 'whether his circumstances are embarrassed'; certification and accommodation of conference delegates; the powers of the conference *vis-a-vis* the constituent circuits; travelling preachers' stipends - and so on, amounting to sixty minuted items in 1820. A strong feature is a certain puritanical strictness, reminiscent in some ways of John Wesley:

> Tobacco -- No preacher who is a smoker of tobacco shall be taken on the Annual Meeting list [Tunstall, 1828]

> In what dress shall our members in office appear in public?
> A. In a plain one; the men to wear single breasted coats, single breasted waiscoats, and their hair in its natural form: and not to be allowed to wear pantaloons, fashionable trowsers, nor white hats. [Hull, 1820]

The records of the various forms of Methodism in all their local, regional and national fora make up one of the richest sources for the history of non-Anglican Protestantism in England and Wales. The decisive severance of Methodism from the Church of England after John Wesley's death, along with the emergence of more 'Dissenting' forms such as Primitive Methodism, allow us to place these sources firmly within our survey of the archives of Nonconformist and Dissenting churches.

## Notes to Chapter 4

1. *Two Calvinistic Methodist Chapels 1743-1811. The London Tabernacle and Spa Fields Chapel*, ed. Edwin Welch, London Record Soc., xi (1975), p. vii ff.

2. *Ibid.*, pp. 11-12, 16-17, 21-2 , 24, 25.

3. For this section: *ibid.*, pp. 2, 3, 5-6, 7, 8, 9-11, 13, 14-15, 21, 25, 47, 48, 50, 71-4, 81-2, 92 ff.

4. The Colne 'new' chapel, with ashlar facade, planned to accommodate 1200 people, cost £115 -10s. With Methodism's emergence out of the Church of England, eventually to take its place as the 'new

Nonconformity', its members, increasingly regarded by the authorities and by themselves, as Dissenters, needed to qualify under the Toleration Act by registering their chapels, so that the documentation accompanying registration became part of the archives of Methodist societies. The first explicitly Methodist licence in Wiltshire dates from 1756: Chandler, ed. *Wiltshire Meeting House Certificates,* p.27.

5,      R. Fieldhouse and B. Jennings, *A History of Richmond and Swaledale* (London and Chichester, 1978), p. 346.

6.      William Jessop, *An Account of Methodism in Rossendale and the Neighbourhood;...* (Manchester and London, n.d. [1880?]), pp. 129-130.

7.      Rupert Davies *et al.,* eds *A History of the Methodist Church in Great Britain* (4 vols., London, 1965-1988), vol. iv, p. 491, 340-1.


**Sources for Chapter 4**

References in this chapter include the following printed and manuscript sources: *Two Calvinistic Methodist Chapels,* ed E. Welch,London Rec. Soc., xi (1975); *Minutes of the Methodist Conference From the First, Held in London, By the Late Rev. John Wesley, A.M., In the Year 1744* (12 vols., London 1812-1855; J.R.L.: The York District Minutes, Commencing from May 24th 1796, Nottingham District Wesleyan Methodist Church, District Minute Book, 3 vols., 1792-1835, vol. I, Minutes of the Whitehaven District Commencing July 8th 1801; L.R.O.: Colne [Lancs.] Methodist Circuit: Circuit Accounts and Finance Papers 1810-1841: Quarterly Account Book, Darwen [Lancs.] Methodist Circuit ... Darwen Circuit Baptisms; B. Moore, *History of Wesleyan Methodism in Burnley and East Lancashire* (Burnley, 1899); L.R.O.: Colne St. John Methodist Church: Accounts and Finance Records 1772-1825, Minute Book for the Methodist Chapel Colne Decr. 4th 1815, Rakefoot [Lancs.], Methodist Church, Crawshawbooth, 1: Steward's Book, 1811; J.R.L.: *Minutes of Conversations between Preachers and Representatives from the Societies in the Methodist New Connexion,* 8 vols., 1797-1807, *Minutary Records: Being Rules, Regulations and Reports, Made and Published by the Primitive Methodists* (Leeds, 1854)

There is an immense amount of material in print for John Wesley, including *The Works of John Wesley,* with sermons, hymns and letters, editor-in-chief Frank Baker, commenced by O.U.P. in 1982 and in progress with Abingdon Press of Nashville, Tenn. For Wesley's letters, the eight-volume edition by J. Telford, London, 1931: see also George Whitefield's *Journals* (London, 1960), and for a later period, *The Early Correspondence of Jabez Bunting 1820-1829,* ed. W. R. Ward, Camden Fourth Series, xi (1972). An excellent collection of documents compiled by John A. Vickers, along with a comprehensive bibliography of Methodist history by Clive D. Field, are in volume iv (1988) of *A History of the Methodist Church in Great Britain,* edited by Rupert Davies *et al.* (4 vols,

London 1965-1988). For brief guides to Methodist records, see: O.A. Becker-legg, 'Methodist Records', *Archives*, v (1961), pp. 8-9; Edwin Welch, 'The Early Methodists and their Records', *Journal of the Society of Archivists*, iv (1971), pp. 20-211; William Leary, 'The Methodist Archives', *Archives*, xvi (1983-4); and E. A. Rose, 'Methodist Records', in Morris Garratt, ed., *Sure Coffers. Some Sources for the history of religion in the North West* (Knowsley, 1987), pp. 25-32.

Some selected examples of Methodist material in central, county and local record offices and libraries include:

P.R.O.: for Cornwall: registers, of baptism and some burials, generally from Methodist circuits and including variants of Methodism such as the Bible Christians, from 1794 to 1837.

P.R.O.: for Devon: baptisms and two burial registers, generally from circuits - Wesleyan and some Bible Christian - mostly early 19th century to 1837.

P.R.O..: for Dorset and Somerset: 4 early 19th-century Wesleyan and Bible Christian baptism registers.

P.R.O.: for Lancashire: 6 Manchester baptismal registers for the period 1801-1837, plus early 19th-century correspondence of the Manchester Methodist Francis Harris to Home Secretary Sidmouth.

In Lancashire Record Office: Colne, Lancs., Circuit Minutes, 1822-23, ac-counts, 1810-98, plans, 1822-68; Colne, Albert Road W., trustees' minutes, 1789-1806, 1815-37, seat accounts, 1777-1886, leaders' accounts, 1778-1868; Rakefoot W. stewards' books, 1811-58; Whalley class books, 1813-1904, circuit plans, 1818-98.

In Essex Record Office: Records of Brightlingsea (Wesleyan) Church, 1822-57, plus catalogues of records of 17 West Ham churches and circuits from 1826 and records of Woods Yard Chapel from 1826.

In Champness Hall, Rochdale: Minutes of Rochdale Wesleyan Leaders' Meet-ing, 1828-60; Cash Books of Union St. Chapel, 1792-1826; Seat Rents Account Book, 1824-44.

In Rochdale Central Library: Journal of transactions in Rochdale Circuit, 1813-34, Rochdale Sunday School Entry Book, 1817-19, Minutes of Rochdale Sunday school teachers' meetings, 1802-19.

In Chetham Library, Manchester: Minutes of Manchester Sunday school com-mittee, 1784-1839.

In Liverpool Methodist Central Hall: Minutes of Liverpool Wesleyan Quarterly Meeting, 1802-1826; Minutes of Liverpool South Quarterly Meeting, 1826-55; Minutes of Mount Pleasant Chapel trustees meeting, 1814-51; Minutes of

Stanhope St. Chapel trustees meeting, 1826-60 (plus other Stanhope St. material from the late 1820s).

In Manchester Methodist Central Hall: Minutes of Irwell St. Chapel trustees' meeting, 1826-46; Minutes of London Road Sunday School, 1811-50; Minutes of Manchester District Meeting, 1825-38.

In Plymouth Grove Methodist Chapel, Manchester: Grosvenor St. Wesleyan Quarterly Meeting minutes, 1824-65.

As well as extensive material on John Wesley, the Methodist Archives at the John Rylands Library, Manchester have sources on other individual Methodists, such as the correspondence, autobiography and conference journal of the minister Charles Atmore (1759-1826), the correspondence of the minister, Joseph Benson (1749-1821), the journal of the Primitive Methodist founder, Hugh Bourne (1772-1852), and the correspondence of the preacher, Samuel Braburn (1751-1816).

# CHAPTER V

## RECORDS OF THE PRESBYTERIAN AND UNITARIAN CHURCHES

### Introduction

In any study of English Presbyterianism and its archives, hard-and-fast denominational labels have to be applied with great caution. Except as the term for an increasingly modified (both ecclesiologically and theologically) tradition, after the Restoration and in the course of the 18th century, even the title 'Presbyterian' is hardly appropriate for that particular variant of Nonconformity, if only because the highly articulated federal system which the term implies, in Scotland for example, existed at best only imperfectly in England. After 1662, Presbyterianism, which had its distant origins in the reign of Elizabeth and which in the 1640s gained and then lost its best opportunity to set up a national system in England, tended to become almost a kind of Independency: 'all the Presbyterians are growing Independent', a leading royalist-Anglican politician wrote perceptively in 1671. This approximation facilitated the exchange of preachers between Independent and Presbyterian congregations, encouraged the temporary merger known as the 'Happy Union' in the 1690s and stimulated various local amalgamations and close collaborations.

Following the rapid break-up of the 'Happy Union', in the early 18th century the Presbyterians' 637 congregations outnumbered those of any other Nonconformist group except the Quakers. In terms of numbers of members, the denomination may have reached nearly 180,000, emphatically exceeding all other Dissenters put together. Compared with some other groups, their numbers, though, like those of other Nonconformists decidedly and increasingly urban-based, were quite well distributed throughout the country, with particular strong points in Yorkshire and Lancashire, the South-West and the North Midlands. Socially, Presbyterianism had been losing much of its earlier support from the gentry and aristocracy, but instead gained a strong 'middle class' following, including urban leaders in towns such as Nottingham.[1]

Despite signs of strength in early-18th century Presbyterianism, crisis overtook the denomination as, following the decisive Salters' Hall (London) conference in 1719, numbers of Presbyterian pastors and congregations went over to a non-trinitarian theology and 'became Unitarian', leading eventually to an apparent extensive 'demise' of English Presbyterianism.[2] Yet, even as these unitarian developments were taking place, some congregations in which accepted theology was moving or had moved away from the orthodox Calvinism and Trinitarianism set out in the 1646 Westminster Confession, actually began reviving the use of the term 'Presbyterian', in part so as to re-establish continuity with a Presbyterian past. Thus, for example, the records of the meeting at Cross Street, Manchester, which in deeds of 1693, 1732 and 1746 scrupulously avoided any denominational labelling, in 1761 and 1778 at long last adopted the term 'Presbyterian', at a time when the congregation and its pastors had long been markedly Unitarian. Similarly, the Unitarians of Kendal who (like the Unitarians of Lewin's Mead, Bristol) used in their records the open-ended term 'Protestant Dissenters', also combined it with 'Presbysterian', a term they were applying to themselves in the 1840s. In circumstances like these, the word 'Presbyterian' at any point after 1660 is best used to mean something like 'Nonconformists claiming filiation from the Presbyterian tradition'. This could in fact involve the retention of practices from out of that Presbyterian tradition, such as collective ordinations by area ministers, as we shall see below.

### Presbyterian-Independent unity and its documentation

Presbyterians and Independents generally shared a common Calvinist theology. In and after 1660, the Presbyterian federal organisation of churches broke down and individual 'Presbyterian' churches became effectively sovereign or, as it were, 'Independent' churches. As 'Presbyterianism' thus became aligned to Independency, schemes such as Richard Baxter's 1652 Worcestershire Agreement provided blueprints for Presbyterian-Independent unification which was achieved in 1691 on the basis of the 'Heads of Agreement' incorporating the 'Happy Union'.

### The Common Fund

An important result of the conciliatory mood leading up to the Happy Union was the Common Fund set up in July 1690 but disintegrating by 1695. Its minutes, with gaps in the series, are lodged in D.W.L.

Taking account of the 'Poverty of Dissenting Ministers and the inability and backwardness of many places to afford them a meere Subsistence', the Fund was set up essentially to re-distribute Presbyterian-Independent wealth, much of it metropolitan and clerical in origin, in favour of poor provincial ministers and congregations and in the interests of the perpetuation of a trained Reformed ministry. The Fund was equipped with an initial management of seven Presbyterian and seven Independent clerics, along with thirty 'private Gentlemen'. All these managers met, or were supposed to meet, weekly on Monday mornings at the premises of a London Nonconformist publisher and elected a clerical chairman for each meeting. Some 'persons' were appointed treasurers, at least one to be present at every meeting.

The treasurers supervised the work of a 'Writer or Book-keeper',who was paid a generous stipend, and it was ordained 'That Books may be kept of all things done, and of all money rec:d and paid, viz.t a Booke of Entryes of all orders and transactions of the Generall managers and such other Bookes as the Treasurers shall judge most proper & convenient.' Further, it was ordered 'That all Letters relating to this business be brought to the Booke-keeper, and put vpon file' and 'That all persons that bring in any money doe note the time when they rec:d it and of whom, and the particular summe how much, which paper shall be signed by the same person, and put vpon file'. The student will see in these requirements an orderly way of proceeding and recording, as might be expected of a London-based body whose core was made up of well-educated clerics.

The Fund set up subscription lists, the first bringing in nearly £1000, with some of the most impressive contributions, each of £100 or more, being made by a group of seven ministers ejected in 1662. One of the most important functions of the Common Fund was 'to provide for a succession of fitt persons to propogate the Gospell when others were removed', by means of grants to necessitous students for training in the ministry at academies around the country or at universities abroad. The Fund minutes recorded the academic qualifications, or lack of them, of potential ministers. Grants, as high as £25, were paid and minuted, including £5 to a renegade 'Romish priest' and two awards from which the Nonconformist community was to reap immense benefits, one of £10 a year to the future historian Edmund Calamy, 'Student at Vtericht, Holland', and the other of £8 to Isaac Watts, the great Nonconformist hymnodist.

With a view to distributing the Fund's resources to best effect, various surveys were commissioned, including a 'Review of the State of the severall Counties in England and Wales, of what Dissenting Ministers as well fixed as Itinerant, with their particular personall circumstances, are now resideing therein. As also an account of the Townes or places, wherein any meetings are, with what allowance is given to those that Supply them. And what young men there be that are educated in Vniversity Learning'. The result of this kind of surveying was a 46-leaf manuscript report drawn up in 1690-2, seemingly on the basis of reports from named correspondents in the counties. The document, in D.M.L. and reproduced by Alexander Gordon, provides the researcher with an unrivalled picture of Presbyterian-Independent Dissent, its ministry, financing and lay membership, throughout England and Wales in the immediate aftermath of the Toleration Act.

Berks

| Ministers that haue a Competent Supply | | Dr. Samson and Mr Cockerell |
|---|---|---|
| | has 4 or 500 hearers the people considerably rich | |
| ...... | | |
| Mr Hardy | Att Newbury has 1000 people as some say, has 501 pr annu | |
| ...... [Kent] | | |
| Mr Prig | At Eltham who is so overwhelmed with Melancholly that hee cannot be prevailed with to preach, though to the Smallest number of hearers, and by this is forgotten of many who might otherwise be helpfull to him, nor will he make known his wants, though he has not a morsell to eate. | |

In the spirit of the Happy Union, denominational tags were largely suppressed, but it was in the nature of Nonconformity's demography at the time that Presbyterian ministers and congregations should preponderate in the survey overall. The picture given of these two fused branches of English Calvinist

Dissent can vary sharply, from large, lively congregations with well supported ministers to the isolation and desperation of provincial congregations and their ministers struggling simply to survive.

Partly under pressure from the quite dogmatically congregationalist Independent revivalist, Richard Davis, the Happy Union broke up in the mid-1690s and its disruption was accompanied by that of the Common Fund. A Congregational Fund was initiated in 1695 but the term 'Common Fund' continued to survive as what was now in effect a Presbyterian Fund, taking that title in 1771 and again in 1784. Confusingly from our point of view, the Minutes of the Common Fund continued for some time after 1696 to record grants to Independents, including one to a manager of the Congregational Fund.

Despite the break-up of the Happy Union at the metropolitan level, Presbyterian-Independent clerical area associations continued to exist after the mid-1690s. We considered the records of the most important of these, the Exeter Assembly of Divines (1691) in Chapter 1.[3] In Lancashire, a body similar to the Exeter Assembly, the Lancashire Provincial Assembly, came into existence in 1693 and brought together clerics identified as Presbyterian and Independent at the time when the Happy Union was distintegrating. The Lancashire Assembly was subdivided into four *classes*, a rather misleading term since in traditional English Presbyterian parlance a *classis*, or classical presbytery, was an area grouping of lay elders and pastors, of the Presbyterian persuasion. Lancashire's *classes*, made up only of clerics but coming from Independent as well as Presbyterian backgrounds, covered the areas of Manchester, Warrington, Bolton and the Northern part of the county. One of these classes, known as the Warrington Classical Meeting, assembled by alternation in a group of South-West Lancashire towns centred on Liverpool and joined the other conferences in its group in sending its two representatives to the county's 'Provincial Meeting'. Laconic and formal for the most part, its minuted proceedings (in transcript, at D.W.L.) are heavily concerned with testing, approving and attemping to control local ministers:

[Liverpool, April 1719]
> Then Mr Henry Winder was admitted a member of this Class, upon his making an acknowledgement of his breaking in upon the rules of it, in the way & manner of his Coming to Leverpoole.

[St Helen's, August 1719]
> Then agreed by this class that the Candidates that offer themselves to examination shall pray, as well as discourse from a text of scripture.

Entries also provide insights into the role of a classis as an arbitrator of disputes within congregations, for example over the fierce divisions in the Manchester Presbyterian Park Lane Chapel over accepting or rejecting the ministry of one Mr. Gardner:

[St Helen's, February 1722]
> The People were exhorted to Peace and a Christian Behaviour towards

one another: To have Days of Prayer together and the dissatisfied were disswaded from withdrawing and advised to wait further to try if they cou'd meet with more Satisfaction in Mr. Gardner's Ministry.

These valuable minutes also throw some light on current events, in particular an outbreak of plague at Liverpool, and a traditional 'puritan' response to it:

[Liverpool, December 1727]
> Then agreed that a Day of Humiliation be observed upon account of the plague at Castle Hey Chappell in Leverpool...

## The Presbyterian congregation

Since Presbyterians in English Presbyterianism's heyday dominated a national assembly, the Westminster Assembly of Divines, and since non-English models, such as the Scots, had highly developed national organs, it may seem surprising that for most of our period the English Presbyterians had no national forum analogous to those of the Friends, the General Baptists and Methodists, that is until the formation of the British and Foreign Unitarian Association in 1825. Thus, for most of the period of this survey, Presbyterianism's basic unit was the individual congregation, of which there were an estimated 637 in early 18th-century England, with, for example, 42 in Lancashire, 46 in Yorkshire, 48 in Somerset, and 38 in London and Middlesex (but none in Bedfordshire or Monmouthshire). The minute books and other books of record, finance and registration from congregations in the Presbyterian-Unitarian tradition can be found in a number of locations, including county record offices: the Greater London County Record Office, for example, has the Brentford Unitarian (later Congregational) Church Book. Two major London archives, Dr Williams's Library and the United Reformed Church Library, contain important Presbyterian-Unitarian material: the latter holds important London sources, including: Founders' Hall, Sessions Minutes 1717-1771, Cash Book 1754-1765, and Baptismal Registers 1689-1773; Oxenden Church, Cash Books 1786-1846 and Swallow Street Sessions Minutes 1734-1807. Serial record books such as the last mentioned are, obviously, of particular value for the long over-view they provide for the student.

A few general, and indeed impressionistic, observations may be offered about Presbyterian-Unitarian church records, especially in contrast with the records of other denominations. In the first place, records of the Presbyterian tradition have less space to devote to discipline - certainly less than some of the stricter sects like the Baptists and Quakers. In compensation, Presbyterian records afford more room to practicalities such as building maintenance and finance.

The relative absence of disciplinary (if not of doctrinal) considerations may be accounted for in one of two ways. First, it may be that the Presbyterians, the least sectarian and hence the least morally perfectionist of the Nonconformist churches, retained vestigial aspirations to a kind of inclusive social membership on the parish model, this precluding an over-rigorous discipline. The second possibility is that the Presbyterians, true to their disciplinarian traditions, did take moral oversight quite seriously (if not quite as seriously as, say, the Quakers), but that discipline was not handled by the church and formally recorded but dealt with by pastors and not entered in church books. That second scenario would certainly accord with the high importance given to ministry in Presbyterian churches and their descendants. The collapse of federal presbyterianism in 1660 and the interest shown in Richard Baxter's 'rectoral' view of the pastor as an authoritative congregational leader, plus the generally high educational attainments of clerics in this tradition, all meant that ministers loomed large in the lives of Presbyterian congregations. This prominence is certainly reflected in church records, which are heavily taken up with the appointments, resignations, deaths, doctrines and financial maintenance of pastors.

Under this head, we should also note how much of the whole Presbyterian-Unitarian archival corpus is taken up with the personalities, letters, lives and doctrines of ministers. Dr Williams's Library is a particularly rich source here. It contains a wealth of Unitarian material with an excellent chronological spread: Miscellaneous Letters of Unitarians, 18th and 19th centuries, with sermons and papers, 1738-1877 (D.W.L., 24.81); Miscellaneous Letters of Unitarians etc. 1783-1877 (D.W.L., 24.86); Letters of Unitarians, 1791-95 (D.W.L., 24.92); Papers, including letters of Unitarians (Priestley, Price, shorthand and longhand, 18th and 19th centuries (D.W.L., 24.107); and Priestley Letters (D.W.L., 24.108). See also the earlier Papers of Michaijah Towgood (1700-1792), a Devon-based Presbyterian-Arian minister and prolific author (D.W.L., 24.60).

Material of this nature in other collections includes the following: at Manchester College, Oxford, Letters and Lectures (on, *inter alia* , ecclesiastical history) by the Unitarian minister, Thomas Belsham (1750-1829); Letters to the Unitarian Minister, Lant Carpenter (1780-1840), and the Correspondence of the Unitarian Minister of Essex St. Chapel, London, Theophilus Lindsey (1723-1808); at the John Rylands Library of the University of Manchester, the three volumes of Correspondence of the Unitarian minister, James Hews Bransby (1783-1847); at Liverpool Record Office, Letters to the Unitarian Minister Nicholas Clayton (1730-1797); at Cambridge University Library, Correspondence and Miscellaneous Papers (about 350 items) of the Unitarian Minister, William Frend (1757-1841); and at University College, London, the Correspondence of the Unitarian writer, Timothy Kenrick (1759-1804).

**Procedures for the appointment of pastors**
The importance of ministers in congregations in the denominational tradition we are considering here is clearly reflected in the amount of space accorded in local church records to issues concerning church ministry. Matters recorded include: how congregations made their choices of pastors; what role neighbouring clergy and area bodies had; what part doctrinal developments and discords had in the appointment of ministers; contracts and conditions of service and the formal record of ordinations.

The record of the procedures of appointment might begin with the formal notification of the resignation, on grounds of ill-health, old age or transfer, of an existing minister. Alternatively, the death of a minister, as at Lewin's Mead church, Bristol, in 1751 when the pastor's death saw the church 'putt into mourning', would instigate a search for a successor: at Lewin's Mead the various steps in the search were carefully recorded by the 'church managers' in their Vestry meeting and its minutes. Following the end of a pastorate, a number of vital administrative measures needed to be taken and entered in the Vestry Room minute book: when a minister retired with an agreed pension, the added burdens of maintaining him along with his successsor had to be shouldered; death necessitated the recruitment of supply preachers and might also make the church both an executor for a deceased minister's charitable bequests and also responsible to his main executors for money due to him from the church.

The church minute books throw light on the routes by which ministers came to congregations. Populous congregations often had assistant ministers (and even, perhaps, additional ministers of the Lord's Supper) and from these assistants a choice might be made of a new minister to succeed one deceased. At Manchester's Cross Street meeting, for instance, on the death of the revered Henry Newcome in 1695, his former assistant, Mr. Chorlton, was called to succeed him, a promotion requiring the appointment of a fresh assistant. Alternatively, a congregation might select a minister from another congregation, perhaps an assistant, to transfer and become its 'main' minister. As for training of recruits, the mainstay was, predictably, the Academies that the Presbyterians ran as seminaries for the ministry: to take just one example out of many, the famous Academy run by the minister Caleb Rotheram (1694-1752) at Kendal was a wellspring of post-trinitarian theology in the North. The Scottish universities provided academic opportunities of a kind from which Presbyterians in England were debarred under the 1662 Act of Uniformity. One possible preparatory training sequence for the ministry was from an Academy to a Scottish university: Presbyterians in Manchester, for instance, recorded their sponsorship of a local boy through the Kendal Academy and the University of Glasgow and their eventual adoption of him as their minister.

Given the high importance and authority of ministers in Presbyterian congregations, it was entirely in order to chose and examine candidates with great care and much prayer for guidance in 'the Choice of Such a Godly Pastor as will be most Instrumental in promoting serious holyness, Vital Religion, and the Edification of precious Souls' as the Lewin's Mead Vestry Room minute book put it. To aid with the search, the views of existing ministers in other congregations might be sought; the community in Whitehaven in West Cumberland used the convenient proximity of Scots Presbyteries to help them make their choice, minuting their overtures in their formal Session Book.[6]

The quest of a congregation to obtain a particular candidate who had been selected and screened did not always come to fruition. At Park Lane,Manchester, in 1799-1800, the congregation split between two candidates and, in the course of the dispute, a trustee absconded with the chapel key. On the theological front, the intensification of Unitarian trends, especially after 1800, added a further complicating factor to the search for ministers: the trustees of the Lancashire

Cockey Moor Chapel, at some point in 1813-1814, sought the advice of a neighbouring minister in a district where the 'old Presbyterian system' still survived, pleading with him to assist in their quest for a pastor capable of:

> healing any discords which have already or may hereafter arise among us, ... we wish to guard against the extreme of Calvinism on the one hand; as well as to discard those Unitarian principles on the other, which have created such animosities in our community: ...
>       We desire to sit under a minister who will keep off peculiar sentiments, and meddle none with interpolations, a plain practical serious heartsearching preacher ...

The letter from which the above excerpt is taken was recorded in a collection of documents relating to 'doctrinal differences' within the congregation at that time, the *Paper Book of minutes... 1813-1814* (L.R.O.).

Consultation with existing ministers might also include the advice of a pastor about his successor, pending his own formal retirement; indeed, it was, naturally enough, not unknown for a respected minister in place to sway the choice of his successor. When the results of various consultations were put together, a formal minute on a decision arrived at might be entered in the church records, in the case of Lewin's Mead in the Vestry Minute Book:

> At several meetings held here from time to time the Reverend Mr. Furneaux hath been Unanimously Nominated to have the Charge and Pastoral Care of this Church and having likewise had the joint Approbation of Several Eminent Ministers Convening with us therein. It is this day ordered that intimation be made next Lord day for our Immediate procedure to issue a Call after the Service of the Afternoon is over.[4]

The 'Call' was the next stage, issued in a letter to the candidate, a copy of which might be enrolled in a church minute book:

> To the Revd Mr Philip Furneaux
> Minister of the Gospel in London_____
> Wee the UnderSubscribed Members of or belonging to the Religious Society or Congregation of Protestant Dissenters ... having Solemnly Implored the Divine Guidance in the Choice of a fitt Person to succeed in the Pastoral Oversight and Care of this Church. And being now Assembled for that purpose we have been Providentially Directed and influenced to make Choice of you Sir with unanimity to succeed in the present Vacant Pastoral Charge of this Church ...

If accepted, a formal 'call' required a letter of acceptance, a copy of which might, again, be recorded in church minutes:

> My Christian Brethren, _____ I thank you for the invitation which you have kindly presented to me to become your minister and pastor; and

I cordially accept the same ...

Such acceptance might be developed into reflections on the minsterial office. However, there was, of course, no guarantee that a call would be accepted. When a designated choice of minister declined the invitation, the protracted procedure of search had to begin again, with further extensive recorded transactions dealing with references ('his whole Deportment in life was becoming the Gentleman the Scholar and the Gospel Minr'), the decision on and issue of a fresh call and, it was to be hoped, its acceptance. A penultimate recorded stage in the recorded business was the inclusion of agreed terms on the practicalities of the appointment:

> Condishons, He is to keep the building and eaverthing in as good repare as he found them, which are at this time as good as they posable can be, Having cost upwards of £70.

As far as the record is concerned, the final formal stage in this necessarily lengthy process was a combination of academic examination, ordination and induction. The sequence and the way it was recorded is seen at its most highly developed with the induction of a minister taking up his first cure. This final part of the routine of ministerial appointment seems to have been put into the hands of colleges of existing settled ministers, where these existed. In a Yorkshire ordination in 1687, a panel of three of these ministers acted as oral examiners for three candidates and conducted tests on scripture knowledge, scriptural languages and philosophy, with verbal defence of a thesis by each of the candidates. There followed a confession of faith, further professional tests and then the laying on of hands, sermon and prayer, with individual ministers being deputed beforehand to particular tasks within the protracted rite. In 1756 at Kendal, where the learned Dr Caleb Rotheram had taken the local church in an Arian direction and made his Academy a centre of scientific study and research, the minuted arrangements for the ordination of his son, also named Caleb (1738-1796)[5], as his successor show how presbyterial forms were continued alongside the evolution of post-Calvinist theology. By considering the record from the clerical side, as we have so far looked at such records from the congregational side, we can see the dovetailing of the role of the congregation, which called the minister, and that of a group of clergy organised in an area synodical body which formally installed him. The record of this installation formed a separate manuscript, included now with the Kendal Unitarian corpus in C.R.O. (WDFC/U). At a meeting, attended by eight ministers, of the 'Provincial Meeting of the Ministers of the Protestant Dissenting Congregations in Cumberland', after a sermon on an appropriate text, one of their number submitted the 'unanimous choice' of Rotheram by the Kendal congregation as their new minister, Rotheram 'produced Testimonial' which was approved by the Provincial body and detailed arrangements were made for the ordination ceremony. To prepare academically for his induction, Rotheram was assigned a scholastic-style *quodlibet* on a topic to do with predestination, along with a sermon text and notice in advance to deliver a profession of faith and answer questions put. Individual ministers were allotted their tasks in the forthcoming ceremony, on 25 August Rotheram passed his various tests, approval was expressed, Rotheram submitted a formal petition from the Kendal congregation for the 'Provincial' to ordain him and finally, on 26 August, Mr Rotheram 'was sett apart to the sacred office of the Ministry by prayer, and the laying on of hands of the Ministry present', and the new minister was given a signed testimonial. It has to be said that all this represents a splendid, but soon to be outmoded, example of classic Presbyterian forms: first, laying on of hands fell into disfavour and at Cross Street, Manchester, ordination itself, before the end of the 18th century, became an option waived by new entrants.

### Church discipline

On the face of it, church discipline does not seem to be a dominant concern in Presbyterian records, a feature that distinguished the churches in the Presbyterian tradition from others, such as those Baptist congregations where the discipline of individuals is a primary item of recorded business, at times almost to the exclusion of all others. However, to say that church discipline seems to feature less in Presbyterian records is not to say that it does not feature at all. There are differences in the amount of space various congregations gave to disciplinary questions and these differences may be partly regional and social. For instance, the records of the church in Whitehaven, in Cumberland and perhaps open to Scots influence, feature discipline quite prominently. The church recorded censure on a man whose son was born three months after his marriage, dealt with an unmarried girl who was pregnant and who had aggravated 'the exceeding sinfulness of her sin' by receiving Communion, and rebuked various forms of sabbath-breaking such as buying and selling: the kind of judicial disciplinarianism reminiscent of the aspirations of the English Presbyterians in their mid-17th century golden age.

Although moral discipline thus seems to loom quite large in the recorded proceedings of the far northern congregation in Whitehaven, the same topic is largely absent from the records of a large southern community, the Lewin's Mead church, Bristol: in that respect, the Bristol congregation may have been more typical of the general run of English Presbyterian and Unitarian societies for most of our period. A rare disciplinary case recorded in the Lewin's Mead Vestry Book is a bare entry to the effect that a couple found to be defrauding the church's philanthropic funds are simply dropped 'from the Monthly Collections list', the written schedule for charity payments: the punishment fits the crime, no more, no less.

Such relative indifference to moral discipline would seem to bear out an observation about the London Presbyterians in 1732 to the effect that they 'very rarely if ever as a church enquire into the conduct and behaviour of their members', and that 'for want of proper discipline immoral persons are continued in their societies'; this would certainly imply that discipline would not be likely to feature prominently as a topic in Presbyterian church records, for instance, in the King's Weigh House Church book, 1699-1795 (D.W.L.), where there was but one recorded disciplinary case in 47 years. However, we have already seen that the topic does figure in the Whitehaven record, and Dr Watts finds evidence of quite intense disciplinary activity in the Registers, 1690-1723, of the High Pavement church, Nottingham (Nottingham University Library) and in the Brentford Presbyterian Church Book (Greater London R.O.). In addition, the

Exeter Assembly Minutes (see above, Ch.1) dealt with the disciplinary oversight of clerics and on one occasion at least of a layman. Even so, it would seem that the control of discipline by Presbyterian pastors, rather than by the congregation as a whole, obviated some of the need to record the application of such discipline as was being implemented; as Dr. Watts writes, '... since [discipline] was usually exercised by the minister, ... there was consequently no need for acts of discipline to be recorded as they were in the minute books of Baptist and Congregational meetings'.[6]

## Church management

Many of the extant records of Presbyterian and Unitarian churches are those of management and trusteeship bodies and are concerned, sometimes quite literally, with nuts and bolts. Although the frequent absence of 'religious' topics may sometimes surprise us, we need to remember that a management committee or a premises committee is just that, and not a doctrinal seminar or a devotional sodality. We shall deal with the documentary record of management in the churches of the Presbyterian-Unitarian affiliation according to the following categories:
(1) charity; (2) general finance; (3) buildings and furnishings; (4) administrative relations with ministers and (5) miscellaneous business.

### (1) Charity

While it is true that Presbyterians and their heirs showed few inhibitions about using the normal social provisions of parish relief, it is also clear from the records of the churches in this tradition that they had their own charitable provisions which, normally, were all the more ample the wealthier a congregation was in its overall composition. At Lewin's Mead, Bristol, charity was dealt with alongside the other varied responsibilities of the Vestry and entered into its minutes. This area included a recorded collection for 'Indigent and Distres'd County Ministers', a list of twelve recipients of £10 left for charity by a deceased minister, the accounts of the yield (£30-4-6d) of a charity sermon in aid of York College, reports of 'Stock' invested for such charitable purposes as an alms house (£3000), the Poor of Lewin's Mead Meeting (£515), and £500 for 'poor Dissenting ministers', the records clearly indicating a large, affluent, socially responsible and financially well managed congregation.

### (2) General finance

Financial transactions of a varied nature occupy considerable space in the records of Presbyterian and Unitarian churches, especially, of course, in those of their boards of trustees and other bodies set up to handle such matters. Lewin's Mead had its own treasurer who, with a couple of other members, entered up properly audited accounts. The Vestry of the same church, attended usually by three to seven individuals, paid bills for the church building, set rents for its landed property, dealt in government stocks and received burial fees. At Kendal the congregation kept a separate account for its rent receipts from, and maintenance expenditure on, its property in the town shambles, while a 'Cash-Book' contained details of quit rents and subscriptions towards building repairs and the minister's salary, along with a separate page of subscriptions for 'Enlarging the Burying Ground'. Indeed, lists of subscriptions form a major item in these sources, subscriptions being opened up for particular schemes, above all for building plans and repairs. Sums subscribed might vary from a shilling to £15 and they provide much valuable information on the numerical size, social composition and identities of the members of the congregations.

*(3) Buildings and furnishings*
For much of the period of this survey, Presbyterian-Unitarian churches retained much of what the 19th century historian of Lancashire Nonconformity, writing of the post-1745 Warrington meeting house, called 'the true Presbyterian style of architecture ... puritanic', a plain and utilitarian architectural aesthetic precluding heavy attention to stylistic detail. It seems that a good deal of the work concerned with drawing up plans was entrusted to professionals of the kind the Lewin's Mead church called 'Mason to the Meeting'. In 1723 the minister at Padiham, Lancashire, John Ashworth, recorded spending only £5-12s on church 'Plans, Specifications, &c', compared with £50 on legal documents and over £24 on publicity, travel etc. The 19th century saw considerable rebuilding or replacement of earlier chapels, and plans of earlier replaced buildings, as in the case of the Stand Chapel near Prestwich, Lancashire, built in 1693 and demolished in 1818, were not always made. By way of a sequel, we can see that, as the 19th century progressed, Nonconformists enthusiastically joined in the Victorian passion for elaborately conceived church architecture, the subject occupying considerable space in church records, especially after mid-century.[7]

The documentation produced by bodies, such as the Lewin's Mead Vestry or the Whitehaven church trustees, which managed church quarters and ancillary buildings such as school rooms and their amenities, is, of course, thoroughly practical in its nature: 'An estimate ... for new gates and doors was produced ... Putty & Glass for large Windows' (5s. 9d) ... Timbr & deal for Chapel' (£70), or a 'general meeting of the Society' to discuss the wall behind the Meeting House, or a recommendation that new walls should be left un-plastered to dry out ('if the appearance of rough walls would not intimidate the Ladies') since 'Green walls hastily plastered is an evil'.

As for church furnishings, a love of simplicity inherited from the puritan tradition and extinguished only in the later 19th century precluded much consideration of decoration. However, the centrality of the sermon and the consequent function of meeting houses essentially as auditoria, meant that seats, pews and sitting galleries were of vital importance in the life and administration of the individual church and its records. As with other denominations, seating was an important source of finance, as well as a potential cause of congregational discord to be resolved by trustees, as at Whitehaven, where they drew up lists of pews with their valuations and 'their tenants' names, in order to establish their claims & prevent disputes concerning the same for the future'; at Lewin's Mead a separate committee of nine, with its own extant minutes, was set up for the 'Appointments of Sittings and the redress of Complaints'. The committee drew up a schedule of 86 ground floor and 30 gallery pews, with the names of their tenants and the number of the seats each pew could contain. The location of the pews and seats generated a regular flow of correspondence and lists, containing much information on the demography and sociology of these communities.

*(4) Administrative relations with ministers*

Church trustees and lay members at large were, at least occasionally, involved in theological issues, especially, as we have seen, upon the appointment of new ministers. Generally however, relations between management bodies and ministers were conducted, as far as the written record is concerned, in terms of the practicalities attendant upon appointments, financial support and coping with vacancies.

Conditions for appointment needing to be agreed and carefully minuted included tenure, salary, accommodation, duties, perquisites and pension terms. The provision of salary required not only attention to the needs of the minister or ministers of a congregation but responsibility to the denominational pool, the Presbyterian-Independent 'Common Fund' which in 1771 became officially known as the Presbyterian Fund and which produced minutes (D.W.L.) and continued to assist Independent ministers. Lewin's Mead invested funds (£550 in 1807) for 'the Ministers of Lewins Mead for the time being' and 'for Poor Dissenting Ministers' (£1100). Trustees also had to cope with the practical consequences of the illness of ministers, such as finding and paying temporary replacements.

*(5) Miscellaneous business*

The wide range of recorded business handled by church managers and trustees extended to timetabling church events, relations with outside bodies and the practicalities of worship. At Whitehaven business included fixing agreed days of fasting and humiliation, along with Communion dates, ministerial appointments and discipline. At Lewin's Mead, the trustees dealt with, and recorded in their minute books, everything from a request on the part of the mayor of Bristol that a petition concerning the city's commercial welfare be available for signatures in the church to a review of the state of the choir:

> a paper signed by several individuals offering their services to sing if the present Choir with some exceptions are discharged ... the Committee are clearly of opinion that a material change in the Singing department must take place ...

**Registration**

An important corpus of Presbyterian and Unitarian records consists of the registration of births/baptisms, burials and some marriages. A Plymouth Presbyterian minister opened a register within three months of his ejection in 1662 (until March 1754 public contracts of marriage before witnesses were legally valid) and the Plymouth Presbyterians recorded three marriages in their early register between 1662 and 1670. The Presbyterians in Moretonhampstead, Devon, opened a register following the 1672 Declaration of Indulgence. A few early Presbyterian communities also had cemeteries. As a senior branch of Nonconformity, Presbyterians were sometimes in possession of enviably complete runs of registers, even if the remarkable series from Hindley Chapel, Lancashire, sent to the Registrar General and entered in the 1841 list of non-parochial registers, has to be regarded as exceptional in its chronological coverage, especially of births and baptisms: [8]

| Vol. 1 | Baptisms | 1644-1754 |
| | Burials | 1642-1754 |
| | Marriages | 1644-1677 |
| Vol. 2 | Baptisms | 1786-1813 |
| Vol. 3 | Births and Baptisms | 1739-1836 |

As minister of the Cross Street church, Manchester, Joseph Mottershead kept a complete register of baptisms from the start of his ministry in 1717 to the year of his death 1771. Registration books, impressive, calf-bound volumes clearly intended to resemble parish registers as closely as possible, could be obtained from booksellers. They had captions along the lines of *A register for the Use of Congregations of Protestant Dissenters* and contained pages of printed forms to be filled in, with perhaps some loose-leaf 'Examples of the manner in which the Blanks should be filled up':

> These are to Certify, That _____ of _____ _____ and of _____
> his wife, was born in _____ the Parish of _____ in the county of
> _____ the _____ Day of _____ in the year one thousand eight hundred
> and _____Registered by me (signature     Protestant Dissenting
> Minister)

Details of fathers' occupations are not required on the kind of form cited above, though these are to be found in some other printed registers, as with the type used by a Scots Presbyterian church in London:

> When Born | When Baptized | Child's Christian Name | Parent's Name | Christian | Surname | Abode | Quality/Trade or Profession | By whom the Sacrament was Administered |

Registers as full as these contain valuable information for the social historian, in this case on a metropolitan immigrant community with its profusion of Scots names and congregation of skilled artisans and their families. Some baptismal entries given in registers are, pardonably, rather fuller than others:

> [1827]: 4 Hinza, Son of Marozi and Makhola his wife a nigro boy of the Brihuana tribe apparently about nine or ten years of age living in the family and under the Protection of Thos. Pringle now of Bunhill Row Finsbury in the city of London, late of South Africa, having given satisfactory & delightful evidence of his Knowledge of the Essential and Fundmental Doctrines of Christianity and having solemnly professed his humble but firm faith in the Lord Jesus Christ, in whom there is neither Greek nor Jew, ... bond nor free, was baptized in the house of the above mentioned Thos. Pringle ...

The register books also contain information on deaths and burials, sometimes simply interspersed with the births and baptisms, sometimes on separate pages. Entries are not necessarily merely formal:

> 1722 NB My [Caleb Rotheram's] d: Hannah was the first that I baptized

publicly & her dear Remains were the first that were deposited near the
Meeting House. She slept in Jesus May 15th & and on the 16th.. a pretty
little Garment was laid up in the wardrobe of the Grave to be worn again
at the Resurrection. Blessed be God for the Hope of this.

**Notes to Chapter V**

1.  For the background to Presbyterian history in the period of this survey,
    see Watts, *The Dissenters*, pp. 100-102, 248-9, 268-9, 289-293, 326, 345,
    371-382, 509-510, and C.G. Bolam, Jeremy Goring, H.L. Short and
    Roger Thomas, *The English Presbyterians From Elizabethan Puritanism
    to Modern Unitarianism* (London, 1968).

2.  R.W. Richey, 'Did the English Presbyterians become Unitarians?',
    *Church History*, xlvi (1973), pp. 58-72; J. C. Spalding, 'The Demise of
    English Presbyterianism 1660-1760', *Church History*, xxviii (1959), pp.
    63-83.

3.  Dr. Nuttall has shown that in some counties, parts of counties and groups
    of counties, Presbyterian clerical conferences also operated, for example
    in Wiltshire, Somerset and the West Riding. Occasional area meetings
    included one at Bristol in 1690 attended by delegates from the West
    Country and from farther afield. Cumberland and Westmorland had a
    joint association, which we shall see functioning as a provincial assembly
    conducting an ordination: Geoffrey F. Nuttall, 'Assembly and Associat-
    ion in Dissent, 1689-1831', *Studies in Church History*, vii, eds. G.J.
    Cuming and D. Baker (Cambridge, 1971), p. 297.

4.  For the eminent Rev. Philip Furneaux (1726-1783) whose career so aptly
    illustrates the fluidity of the differentiation between Presbyterians and In
    dependents, see *The Dictionary of National Biography*, vii, pp. 770-2.

5.  Caleb Rotherham, jr., took over from his father in 1756, four years after
    the latter's death: see Cornelius Nicholson, *The Annals of Kendal* ...
    (London and Kendal, 1861), p. 164.

6.  Watts, *The Dissenters*, pp. 321-3.

7.  See, eg., J.E. Jenkins, *History of Unitarianism in Padiham. 1806-1906.
    A Centenary History* (Accrington, 1906), p. 9; R. Travers Herford,
    *Memorials of Stand Chapel* (Prestwich, Lancs. 1893), pp. 49-50; J.C.G.
    Binfield, 'The Building of a Town Centre Church: St. James's Congreg-
    ational Church, Newcastle Upon Tyne', *Northern History*, xviii (1982),
    pp. 153-181.

8.  Nightingale, *Lancashire Nonconformity*, vol. Wigan, Warrington, St.
    Helen's, p. 4; Peskett, *Guide to the Registers of Devon and Cornwall*, pp.
    xxxix, xliii.

**Sources for Chapter V**

References in this chapter are to the following manuscript sources:

C.R.O.: Unitarian Chapel, Kendal, Copy Register of Baptisms and Burials 1687-1838, plus additional local Unitarian material.

D.W.L.: (transcripts) The Minutes of the Warrington Classical Meetings...; Monthly Meeting Minute Books, Vestry Room, Lewin's Mead Meeting, Bristol, 1751-1823; (additional) Lewin's Mead Vestry Minutes, 1807-1823; Lewin's Mead Vestry Book, 1823-1850.

L.R.O.: Cockey Moor Chapel, Paper Book of Minutes ... , 1813-1814.

U.R.C.L.: Session Book of the Associate Dissenting Congregation of Whitehaven, 1787-1882; Whitehaven High Street Trustees Minutes, 1744-1754; Register of Births and Baptisms of the Scots Church, London Wall, Begun January 1822; [Register of] Baptisms Solemnised in the Scotch United Secession Church, Oxenden Street ... [London] in the Year 1834 (The Scots Presbyterian 'Secession Church' was formed in 1733).

In print: Sir Thomas Baker, *Memorials of a Dissenting Chapel, Its Foundation and Worthies*; ... (London and Manchester, 1884); George Fox, *The History of Park Lane Chapel* (Manchester, 1897). Alexander Gordon's *Freedom after Ejection. A Review (1690-1692) of Presbyterian and Congregational Nonconformity in England and Wales* (London and Manchester, 1917) contains the material on the Common Fund and the survey of congregations.

The relevant journals are *The Journal of the Presbyterian Historical Society of England* (from 1973 *The Journal of the United Reformed History Society*) and *The Transactions of the Unitarian Historical Society*. See also J.T. Darling, 'Presbyterian Church of England Records', *Archives*, v (1961), p.6.

Presbyterian-Unitarian material in record offices includes:
Lancashire Record Office: Ainsworth - Minutes and Letters, 1813-14 and deeds, 1719-93; Chorley - abstract of title, 1655-1751, miscellanea, 1755-1839, rebuilding papers, 1803-1928, receipts for teaching expenses (with names of pupils), 1768-1857; Preston - miscellanea, 1706-1971.

P.R.O. : For Devon : Colyton Old, or George's, Meeting, Baptism Register, 1773-1836; Bowden Hill Meeting, Crediton, Baptism Register 1735-1837 (with deeds in the Devon Record Office); Cullompton Baptism Register, 1693-1837, Burials Register, 1693-1837; Dartmouth Baptism Register, 1726-1837; Exeter James' Meeting (later George's Meeting), Baptism Register, 1687-1837, Burials Register, 1748-1837; Hatherleigh Baptism Register, 1729-1789; Honiton Baptism Register, 1697-1837; Ilfracombe, Higher Chapel, Baptism Register, 1729-1837, Burials Register, 1821-1837; Moretonhampstead, Cross Meeting, 1672-1836; Plymouth, Treville St./Norley St. Baptism Register, 1662-1835, Marriage Register, 1662-1670, Burials Register, 1662-1695; Plymouth, Batter St., Baptism Register, 1704-1837, Burials Register, 1768-1837; Sidmouth, Higher or Old Meeting, Baptism Register, 1753-1836; Tavistock, Abbey Chapel, Baptism Register, 1693-1837; Topsham Baptism Register, 1744-1837, Burials Register, 1771-1837; Woodbury and Lympstone, Gulliford Meeting, Baptism Register, 1773-1828, Burials Register, 1786-1836.

# CHAPTER VI

# THE RECORDS OF THE SOCIETY OF FRIENDS

## Introduction

The Society of Friends originated in the welter of religious excitement and innovation in England in the 1640s and 1650s. Though from the beginning a position of leadership was accorded to the 'founder', George Fox (1624-1691), Fox was not the sole creater of Quakerism. The movement arose from a widespread quest in mid-17th century England for a Christianity that was less dogmatically precise and less preoccupied with human guilt and predestination than was the prevailing orthodox Calvinism of the period. Fox and the early Quakers offered a religion that saw the potential for goodness in all men and women. However, the movement was by no means lacking in moral discipline and, though it rejected Calvinistic theology, it inherited and reinforced the traditional strict puritan ethical code.

Quakerism took to its furthest point the love of spontaneity in worship that was characteristic of radical puritanism. Worship was remarkably formless - there were no external sacraments for example - but, in contrast to this liturgical form-lessness, there was a highly formalised system of church government. The Society of Friends was perhaps the most sectarianised body within Nonconform-ity. Not only did it maintain a posture of uncompromising hostility towards the Church of England, but it eschewed institutionalised collaboration with the other Nonconformist bodies and also repudiated some of the demands of citizenship (especially the payment of tithes to the Church of England) as these were understood in the highly confessional state that was early modern England.

The relative obduracy and even radicalism of the Friends meant that they were likely to feature more than other Dissenters in public records (including those of the Church of England) quite apart from their own archives.[1] Random examples from civil records include the 1686 conviction of ten Colchester Quakers enrolled in the Colchester borough sessions records at the Essex Record Office or the Hertfordshire sessions book, 1658-1700, which in 1684 dealt with the 'trial of John Raylett and the other Quakers, indicted for refusing to take the oath of allegiance the second time, ...'.[2] We cannot in this brief survey cover the immense amount of material on Quakers in Church of England records, espe-cially over their refusal of tithes. A glimpse of just one aspect of the Anglican-Quaker legal encounter, as it is recorded in Church sources, can be seen in collections of probate papers normally requiring oaths, which Quakers refused to swear and coming within the purview of the ecclesiastical courts, for example the sets of papers in the Lichfield Joint Record Office and the Nottingham County Record Office.[3] The established Church also carefully monitored the existence and activities of the Friends through periodic enquiries such as the visi-tation articles of Archbishops of Canterbury, Secker (1758) and Moore (1786), in Lambeth Palace Archives:[4]

> Are there any Quakers in your Parish , and how many? Is the Number lessened or increased of late Years, and by what means? Have they a

meeting House in your Parish duly licensed, and how often do they meet there? ...

Such queries paid particular attention to the Quaker refusal to pay tithes. The following, in Lambeth Archives, may be taken as a fairly typical reply from an incumbent to metropolitical enquiries:

...they seem extremely bigotted to their own Opinions and hold their Neighbours in great contempt as if for want of their light, everybody else was in the dark.

Such ministry as the Society of Friends possessed was amateur and self-supporting. Whereas in Nonconformist churches with a high degree of clerical leadership, such as the Presbyterians, much activity must have been undertaken by ministers without written record, the Friends' collective way of conducting their church business in formal, minuted meetings was the single most important factor in ensuring that their actions were recorded with an assiduity not found in any other denomination. At the same time, freed from the necessity to finance a salaried pastorate of ministers attached to and supported by particular congregations or by a central fund, the Society could afford to proliferate its number of individual worshipping communities (with their low-cost buildings) according to demographic and geographic needs. Numerous small units of the Society existed in thinly populated areas like Cumberland and Westmorland, areas to which the Society owed much of its origin in the 1650s. In addition, there were also major urban communities, as at London and Bristol. By 1718, the Quakers had by far the largest number of Nonconformist congregations in England (672 compared with the Presbyterians' 637), but were the second smallest Dissenting group in terms of overall numbers.[5] Numbers continued to fall decade by decade for the remainder of our period and beyond, no doubt because of the rigorous discipline and free use of expulsion.

One expression of Quakerism's strongly etched separate identity was its elaborate organisational structure, perhaps originally devised to withstand the ferocious persecution that the Quakers, as uncompromising radical Dissenters, faced in the years after 1660. The basic unit was the Particular or Preparative, Meeting, an assembly for worship and business. For reasons already given, the number of Preparative Meetings was allowed to expand quite freely, even though a gathering might consist of relatively few adherents. The Preparative Meeting sent representatives to the Monthly Meeting, a district conference for business, discipline and general 'Church Affairs'. Monthly Meeting representatives attended assemblies, generally of Quakers in one county, meeting four times a year, the Quarterly Meeting. Attenders from the counties met in London for a Yearly Meeting, and there were also regional Yearly Meetings. The London Yearly Meeting had an executive committee, the Meeting for Sufferings. There were also important bodies such as the London-based Morning Meeting, which vetted Quaker publications, and the London Six Weeks Meeting, which dealt with expulsions from the Society and some reinstatements, legacies, gifts, denunciations against individuals, and resignations of membership.[6] All these bodies produced their own runs of minute books.

At every level up to Yearly Meeting (and after 1784 at that level too) women Friends had their own business meetings, apart from their menfolk, this giving the Society a double structure of parallel meetings and records. Indeed, Quakers showed remarkable creativity in evolving institutions, such as the 18th-century development of meetings for their semi-clerical Ministers and Elders. There was a considerable amount of travelling from meeting to meeting and, even more, of written contact and communication upwards and downwards in a chain of conferences. Indeed, the sinews that held the Society together were of ink and paper: official and personal letters; directives and questions to be answered, initiatives from meetings often adopted by higher bodies and issuing instructions that were then passed back down the chain; certificates and marriage notices. Materials such as 'Queries' and 'Epistles' from Yearly Meeting, letters to meetings from individual Friends and between Quaker administrators of the Society's business, information from the Quaker schools such as Ackworth, Yorkshire, on their administration, apprenticeship indentures, property deeds, burial and birth notes, notices of expulsion, marriage certificates, and so on, in a vast profusion, were stored, often in safes like the one in the Leeds Meeting House or the safe used to store the rich Lancaster Quaker archive now in the L.R.O.[7] Meanwhile, each body kept its own documentation, at the centre of which were sequences of minute books of proceedings.

### Yearly Meeting

The London Yearly Meeting of the Society of Friends met regularly from the 1670s and was attended usually by Friends suggested by meetings down to the level of the Particular Meetings. The Yearly Meeting exercised a high degree of authority within the Society, including oversight of annual regional meetings of Friends in groups of counties. The Yearly Meeting sent out summaries of its thinking on a whole range of Quaker 'concerns' - relations with the state, non-payment of tithes, rejection of 'heathen' names of days and months, the single-person form of address, simplicity of life-style and so on, often adjusting its rulings so as to take account of new social and cultural developments such as the incipient appeal of fox-hunting to affluent late eighteenth-century Quakers. Monthly and Quarterly Meetings were required to keep the 'Yearly Meeting Papers together in a book', something also done in Particular Meeting minute books. Friends in the Quarterly Meetings were also supposed to read 'the Yearly Meeting papers and to observe with all diligence to put the same in practice...'.[8]

The two to four 'substantial' Friends deputed by each Quarterly Meeting to attend the London Yearly Meeting would return with a 'printed epistle and manuscript, which were read, and also a very full account of the transactions of the Meeting...'. The 'Epistle' was subsequently read out in the district Monthly Meetings and then passed on to the Particular Meetings so 'that they may be in a capacity to answer what is therein recommended against the quarter meeting...', the flow of information and comment thus proceeding from the local cells up through the county structure. The onus of responsibility was for Quarterly Meetings to require the Monthly Meetings to make sure that the Particular Meetings carried out the Yearly Meeting's directives as set out in its annual Epistle. Attenders from Quarterly Meetings at Yearly Meetings brought back with them various specific requirements relating to   Meeting records, for example a 'desire' of Yearly Meetings that Friends in every Meeting compile retrospective lists of persecutions ('sufferings'). Starting in 1682, the oversight of Meetings was regularised in standardised 'Queries' agreed at Yearly Meeting. The first set read as follows:[9]

> 1. What friends in the Ministry, in their respective Counties, departed this Life since the last Yearly Meeting?
>
> 2. What friends Imprisoned for their Testimony have dyed in Prison since the last Yearly Meeting?
>
> 3. How the Truth [i.e. Quaker beliefs] has prospered since the last Yearly Meeting, and how friends are in Peace and Unity?

Ultimately, the queries, from the answers to which it was hoped a regular up-to-date picture of the moral and spiritual state of the whole Society could be assembled, reached their termini in the Particular Meetings. By 1696, eight queries were being asked and more were added later; they came to cover a most extensive range of topics, including Quaker apprenticeships for Friends' children, regular attendance by Friends at Meetings, avoiding worldly ways, keeping out of undue debt, drawing up wills carefully, the provision of Quaker schools, and proper preparation for marriage. Though the written answers were often routine - 'nothing on them but well and the said queries are continued' - the queries were designed to provide the Yearly Meeting, via the Monthly and Quarterly Meetings, with an annual searchlight on the state of the Society.

**Quarterly Meetings**
Though it was sometimes difficult to find Friends, especially in the regions more remote from London, to attend Yearly Meeting, there seems to have been less difficulty in getting representatives for regional Yearly Meetings or for Quarterly Meetings. An important function of the Quarterly Meeting was to act as a 'switchboard' in the constant interchange between the Yearly Meeting above it and the Monthly Meeting below it. The Quarterly Meetings passed on recommendations from the Monthly Meetings to the Yearly Meeting and generated administrative and clerical duties for the Monthly Meetings, from whose representatives they were made up. They collated data on births, marriages and deaths, prodded the Monthly Meeting into investigating the state of the Particular Meetings, arbitrated disputes between Monthly Meetings, especially over poor relief cases, and helped with the management of Meetings' property and trusts, though particularly complex cases might have to be referred to the Yearly Meeting. The minute books of the London and Middlesex Quarterly Meeting (in F.H.L.), extant from 1690, provide an excellent example in detail of what Quarterly Meetings did and what business they recorded. Its 'concerns' included: subscriptions to the Quaker school at Ackworth in Yorkshire; affirmations (the Quakers' alternative to oaths, which their consciences forbade); birth and burial notes; the appointment of Meeting clerks; the 'inconvenience' of coaches at funerals; the avoidance of debate in Yearly Meeting; Friends 'selling what they cannot wear' (i.e. selling fancy clothes); Friends not serving on

inquest juries; the cessation of the earlier practice of compiling narratives of 'Judgements upon Persecutors'; review of 'marriage dinners'; the silencing of ministers who had become insolvent; the liberation of 'People of Colour'; advice against frequenting of taverns and on temperance; data on Quakers' tithes paid vicariously, and so on.

Quarterly Meetings were established from the late 1660s and Quarterly Meeting minute books, the staple records of these meetings, begin in series from around the same point in time. The following are examples of 'runs' of county Quarterly Meeting minute books during the period of this survey: Bedfordshire Quarterly Meeting Minute Books: 8 volumes, 1668-1865 (Herts. County Record Office, Hertford); Bristol and Somerset Quarterly Meeting Minute Books: 7 volumes, 1668-1858 (Somerset County Record Office, Taunton); Wiltshire Quarterly Meeting Minute Books: 4 volumes, 1678-1785 (Wiltshire County Record Office, Trowbridge); Cumberland Quarterly Meeting Minute Books: 4 volumes, 1672-1723 and 1731-1836 (Cumbria County Record Office, Carlisle); Durham Quarterly Meeting Minute Books: 4 volumes, 1671-1834 (Friends' Meeting House, Darlington).

The Quarterly Meeting minute books thus generally form unbroken sequences, the clerk simply opening a new minute book when its predecessor was full. The Meetings recorded in these volumes were well-organised and business-like affairs scheduled well in advance, sometimes adjourned or held over two sessions, and the day's work starting as early as 6.30 a.m. The same representatives tended to serve repeatedly.

The gatherings so far discussed were in fact *men's* Quarterly Meetings, and in accordance with the Friends' principles of the equality of the sexes, women had their own business Meetings, at this as at other levels. It is possible that the women's Quarterly Meetings tended to be less pressed for business and administration than the men's equivalents. Thus, whereas a men's Quarterly Meeting Minute Book might record satisfaction at 'Having gone through much business that concerned this Meeting', the relative absence of practical affairs in the women's Quarterly Meetings may have allowed their sessions to be more reflective in a religious sense: 'here is not much business proposed to the meeting so that, blessed be the Lord, our chief occasion is to wait upon Him, and we are satisfied well therein...'.

## Monthly Meetings

Monthly Meetings, again held in parallel men's and women's sessions, were the hub of Quaker administration. Borrowed, perhaps, from the monthly worship conventions of the Quakers' forebears, the Seekers, Monthly Meetings, the foci usually of about four to seven Particular Meetings, were one of Quakerism's earliest organisational forms and were rapidly established by or in the 1660s. As with the Quarterly Meeting and the Particular Meeting, the basic record of the Monthly Meeting as a business conference was its series of minute books, kept by a succession of clerks. Some of the early Monthly Meeting clerks established high standards of compilation, presentation and penmanship, as with the high-quality copper-plate or 'Italian' calligraphy of Robert Rockhall, the clerk at

Gainsborough, Lincolnshire from 1679 to 1685. A later habit of some Monthly Meeting clerks was to compile one or even two preliminary drafts of minutes, often in pencil and in cheap exercise books, before entering up a final pen-and-ink version in a leather-bound minute book. This custom arose not just out of love for meticulous presentation but because Quaker minutes had to express accurately the agreed sense of the meeting they were recording.

The keeping of Monthly Meeting minute books seems to have arisen from initiatives by Quarterly Meetings: 'Let every Monthly Meeting take care that a boke be provided for every Monthly Meeting wherein what is done at every Monthly Meeting be recorded'. From these, beginning in the 1660s and 1670s, sets of Monthly Meeting minute books continued throughout the period of this survey. In common with some other Dissenter minute books examined in earlier chapters, a Monthly Meeting minute book, or at least the first volume in a series of such, might open with a formal title page or preamble, perhaps containing some religious statement, as in the following case from the (printed) Gainsborough, Lincolnshire, Monthly Meeting minutes:

> A Booke of Records for the Monthly Meeting.. wherein for the Information of such as are concerned is recorded severall things as well of publique as of particular Concernment in relation to the pretious Truth... Here is allsoe recorded seasonable Admonitions & Advise from severall Friends of Truth... wherein may be observed the Continuation of Gods loveing Kindness to Friends....

The extensive business coming before a Monthly Meeting as the fundamental unit of Quaker administration, and recorded in the minuted proceedings of those Meetings, includes (1) charity and poor relief; (2) discipline; (3) 'sufferings' (i.e. data on persecution); (4) finance and property management; and (5) registration of births, marriages and deaths.

*(1) Charity and poor relief*
Quakers tried to use charity as a stimulus to achieving individual self-reliance: hence the importance to them of establishing, subsidising and supervising apprenticeships. They were also careful to establish in writing the charity cases for which Meetings were responsible and there was considerable correspondence between Monthly Meetings on individual charity relief cases.

Apart from the permanent commitment to funding apprenticeships, Monthly Meetings collected monies, and entered the sums collected in Monthly Meeting minute books, especially during the period of intense persecution down to 1687, for distribution among Friends suffering from persecution in various parts of a county. The Monthly Meetings also recorded long-standing commitments to particular named members, especially the aged; arranged for relief recipients to reciprocate by performing useful tasks, such as taking food to imprisoned Friends; considered a scheme, which had some vogue in the 1690s, for setting up workhouse-style 'colleges of industry'; helped fire victims;  gave doles to vagrants;  discharged debtors from gaol;  lent out poor relief funds at interest to members; paid doctors' and apothecaries' bills, and a host of other philanthropic activities. Meanwhile, the main county and local Quaker meetings, Quarterly and Particular, were hardly less active in the orderly administration of charitable work, the Quarterly Meeting dealing more with national causes and with co-ordinating works of charity throughout the counties.

*(2) Discipline*

The main categories of offence covered by Friends' recorded church discipline were debt, when incurred through negligence or extravagance; drunkenness; sexual offences such as unmarried motherhood; and marrying outside the Society. Monthly Meetings were the spearheads of discipline. Their procedures, often protracted, were to interview offenders, seek repentance, and if this was not forthcoming, expel ('disown' or 'deny') the individual in question, usually with a formula about re-admission in case of amendment. The recorded stages can be followed in the following excerpts:

(a) Identification of the individual being disciplined and his/her Quaker credentials:

> Stephen Catley son of Edmund Catley ... having been educated among us the People call'd Quakers, & from his childhood hath frequented our Meetings for Worshipp...

(b) The offence and its antecedents:

> ...but the said Stephen after the death of his father taking indirect courses, ... he entangled himselfe with a woman not of our society, and was joyned to her in marriage by a priest ...

(c) Narrative of attempts made to reclaim the offender:

> ...he was thereupon both privately & publickly advised in severall things relating to his welfare...

(d) Repudiation of the impenitent:

> ...notwithstanding all our good advice and counsel [he remained recalcitrant and] wee ... can do no less than Testifie against him while he remains in that spirit, and his wrong practices & disorderly walking as above; so that what he may wrongfuly act in the said spirit of disorder may not be charged upon us

(e) The possibility of repentance:

> Nevertheless it is our desire, that the Lord may so worke upon him by his judgment as to bring him to a true repentance & amendment of life...

An earlier procedure was for disownments of individuals to be entered in minute books, but later they were recorded in specially prepared documents called 'Testimonies of Denial' or 'of Disownment'. A copy of such a testimony was sent to the disowned, another copy was read out in his Meeting and was then usually, but not invariably, entered into the minutes.

### (3) 'Sufferings'

The Quakers were anxious to record the various privations they underwent, chiefly in the forms of fines, distraints and imprisonments, both before and after 1689, largely on account of their refusal to pay tithes. Friends seem, originally at least, to have compiled persecution records as a gesture of confrontation: 'as a testimony against the murdering spirit of this world...'. Later, with the dawn of toleration from 1687 or 1689 onwards, Friends may have intended the compilation of sufferings with a view to enlisting sympathetic opinion which would lead to an alleviation of burdens. There was a repeated insistence on drawing up detailed and accurate accounts of Quakers' privations which were eventually published in Besse's *1743 Sufferings of the... Quakers*. The manner of entering the accounts of sufferings was described in some detail by Yearly Meeting:

> That exact accounts and true record be kept of all sufferings for truth, tythes and all other Sufferings for Truth, whether by distress [distraint], sequestration, or imprisonment as full and complete in all respects as possibly may be, with their dates and the time of comencement of suits and the value of what is taken and by whom and for whom, and also of deliverances, and a speedy account given when any Friends are discharged from imprisonment or proceedings against them stopped... and that a distinct account be kept of sufferings, upon what statute or by what ways or means sufferings are brought upon Friends.

Hardships arising from Friends' refusal to swear oaths were recorded separately. Another category of record under the general heading of 'sufferings', though falling out of fashion after the seventeenth century, was the detailed historical narration of the misfortunes of Friends' persecutors:

> thus for the harsh persecuting J.P. George Halstead, the Lord was pleased in His judgement [to bestow] gangrene which began in his toe.. and so went upwards in so much that it stank, and the smell thereof was so offensive that few ... would endure him or to come near him ... till at least it arrived at his heart, [making an end of] that threatening and cruel persecutor...

Friends also entered into their records detailed questions and answers containing legal advice on the avoidance of persecution where this was compatible with conscience.

The Quaker record of persecution, full and exact as it is, forms a valuable source with which to chart the rise and fall in the incidence of religious repression in late 18th and early 19th century England: 'great sufferings' in 'this day of trial' at the height of the Tory Reaction, in 1684, and subsequently a 'bowing time' in a second Tory Reaction towards the end of Anne's reign, and a certain amount of understandable panic in 'a time of trouble and exercise' at the time of the 1715 Jacobite rising. Coping with persecution also generated a considerable amount of financial documentation, including the payment of discreet bribes, in the forms of cash, wine and other presents, to gaolers, justices and others, and even payments to repair the gaol where Friends were lodged.The Monthly Meetings were also the agencies for collecting material in the area in which Friends underwent some of their most acute long-term 'sufferings', the matter of tithes. It was a mark of the uncompromising absoluteness of their separation from 'the world' that Friends refused to make these payments to the Church of England (and to lay impropriators) that other Nonconformists, however grudgingly, paid. Friends were required not just to abstain from payment, and to repudiate debts to well-meaning vicarious payers, but also to say *why* they refused to pay. Their voluminous testimonies against tithes take us into a fascinating world of the consciousness of the ordinary professing Quaker.The Monthly Meetings reviewed, received and collated the 'accounts' that Friends in the Particular Meetings tendered against the 'old and grand oppression' of tithes, with Friends in the Meetings designated to elicit those testimonies in special sessions:

> The Friends appointed at last month meeting to bring account of friends' clearness in their testimony against tithes... give account that there was a time appointed for the same wherein most friends did give in a clear account...

The testimonies were entered in Monthly Meeting records: at Lancaster, for example, they were 'assiduously recorded in a separate volume for the purpose which was later bound with the Monthly Meeting minutes...'. Testimonies also appeared in Quarterly Meeting and Women's Quarterly Meeting minute books: the Yorkshire Women's Quarterly Meeting minute book, 1678-1745, for instance, has eleven pages of such testimonies under 1678.[11]

To help Friends in the local Meetings, copies of model testimonies might be sent down to them, and hence, perhaps, there was a certain thematic stereotyping. Eventually, the testimonies were read out in the Quarterly Meetings after having been 'perfected and digested' in Monthly Meetings.

Part of the purpose of the testimonies against tithes was to assure otherwise ill-informed sympathisers with the Friends' plight that the refusal to pay was conscientious and absolute, and that therefore no reimbursements would be made for those dues paid, by neighbours, relatives and friends, over the heads of the Quakers actually liable for them:

> neither shall I take him to be my friend till he promise to [pay vicarious tithes] no more ... I have a testimony by suffering to bear against that formal worship and house called the church ...

Thus repudiation of payment had to be made as articulate and as intelligible as possible, forming a collective repudiation of tithe paying in terms of Scripture, the work of Christ and church history: tithes were warranted in the Old Testament by Mosiac law, abolished by Christ's 'free' priesthood and, though exacted by the medieval Catholic Church, were to be abrogated in a true Reformation:

Christ the everlasting priest has put an end thereto, and that priesthood is ended wherein they were upheld ... Christ is come and hath fulfilled the law under which tithe was payed .. I believe tithes ought not to be paid in this glorious dispensation we are under ... an antichristian custom introduced by the Pope in the dark night of apostacy, and continued by those who notwithstanding their specious pretence of Reformation are found in the same spirit with them who set up these idolatrous practises by the spirit and power of Antichrist ... [Christ] said I will make a new convenant with my people not according to the old ... [tithes are] against Christianity in these gospel days ... Christ the everlasting priest has put an end thereto and that priesthood is ended where in they were upheld ... we do not read neither do we believe that the apostles either took tithes or payed tithe but as they had freely received they freely ministered ...

As well as allowing Friends to repudiate payments made on their behalf - 'no kindness but a trouble to me' - the statements against tithes reinforced the collective sectarian identity of the Society of Friends and its members' belief in its place in the drama of salvation. Testimonies were also forthcoming from those who were not actually liable for tithe but who joined in this act of collective solidarity by stating on record that they would not pay, even if they were so liable. Alongside the anti-tithe testimonies as such, a sustained quest for information on the value of goods distrained in lieu of tithes revealed a full picture of the financial damage done to the community, as well as numerous narratives of confrontations with parsons, collectors, impropriators, tithe farmers and various agents. Finally, this body of records covering the whole area of anti-tithe testimony was supplemented by a flow of standardised Yearly Meeting documentation sent out to Meetings throughout the country. This embraced legal advice on procedures to be adopted in tithe cases (1695) and regular minutes on maintaining anti-tithe testimony (e.g. 1689-90, 1733, 1752) and on its details and technicalities, such as vicarious tithe payments (1703), impropriated tithes (1703, 1706), statutory relief from tithes (1736), accurate recording of tithe sufferings (1737), and rebates from distraints (1757). It may be the case that, after about the mid-18th century, alterations in Quaker sociology, especially the Society's increasing urbanisation, required less prominence for this area of archival record.

*(4) Finance and property management*
The Monthly Meeting was at the mid point of a chain of Quaker financial and property management. Each Quaker Meeting, at every level, had a float of money known as its 'stock', raised largely by collections and legacies and used to defray expenditure on upkeep of premises, charity and relief payments, outgoings on apprenticeships and schools, legal payments of various kinds, etc. Particular Meetings were the ultimate source for a steady flow of monetary contributions which made their way upwards through the Monthly and Quarterly Meetings to the national level, with the Monthly Meeting acting as the essential intermediaries in the transmission:

A great necessity appearing for a collection for the supply of the National Stock by reason of all the stock being expended and considerable debts being contracted and also other pressing occasions towards relieving poor Friends in severall nations, this [Quarterly] Meeting earnestly desires the severall Monthly Meetings' care and expedition in contributing to the aforesaid occasion ...

Monthly Meetings had, and increasingly accrued, resources of their own in the forms of testamentary bequests of land and investment funds, but, for their own running costs, to avoid deficit and to cover special collections such as the example given above, they had to appeal to the Particular Meetings: on the other hand, Monthly Meetings short of cash for running expenses might borrow from county 'stock' administered by Quarterly Meetings.

The extensive financial administration that went on in Monthly Meetings is documented not just in minute books but in voluminous loose papers covering such matters as: the financial provisions for charity; collections from named individuals (but no 'pew rents'); management of bequests, especially those of real estate; eventually, a steady stream of expense claims from Friends travelling on Meetings' business; outgoings on Friends' increasingly ambitious concern with books and libraries; donations to emerging Quaker philanthropic causes such as anti-slavery; and running costs of premises and schools.

Quaker Meeting houses were the most plain and functional of the places of worship even of the English Dissenting community. Though Friends in country districts still sometimes foregathered in private houses, or otherwise met in modest buildings that were in all respects rustic vernacular constructions, characteristic of their regions in style and materials, the larger urban communities built or enlarged more imposing structures, if only to house area Meetings. Even these buildings, however, were overwhelmingly utilitarian and inexpensive: records of a 1708 'rebuilding' (i.e. extension) of the Meeting house in Lancaster, in part to allow it to accommodate Quarterly Meetings, show it to have cost only just over £177. New Meeting Houses were frequently paid for by carefully recorded cash gifts from Meetings over a wide area. In 1667, minutes of the Men's Meeting in Bristol record an agreement 'that a large publique meeting house on this [i.e. north] side of the bridge bee built on the ground ...', noting the appointment of a group of thirteen to 'consider of, contract for, build; & finish a new large Meeting house with a floor upon the ground in some place on this side of the Bridge ...'. In 1669 they recorded a decision, arrived at by lot, on the siting of the new building, and subsequently minuted structural alterations:

> [1670] Theophelos Nuton is ordered to set up convenient partitions betweene the two meeting roomes to the end the lesser roome may be inclosed for the third days meeting and the greater roome for the 6th days meeting. ...
> or [1675] Friends proposeing the conveniancy of a gallerie on the west side of the meeting house. Upon consideracion thereof this meeting accords that a gallery will be very necessary there, but refers it to be againe considered at the next meeting ... .[12]

Apart from running repairs and alteration, there were few other costs of premises under the Meeting House head , certainly no manses, and burial yards were cheap to maintain. However, especially from about 1690, Friends began to take very seriously, and to record in Meeting minutes, the provision of schools and school-teachers, Monthly Meetings assuming considerable responsibility for these arrangements. In Bristol, Friends' records show a particular early attention to the question of Quaker schooling:

> in 1671 it was proposed to the meeting whether or no there might bee any encouragement of John Toppin, to come to this citty on the score of keeping schoole, & freinds doe desire Geo. Gough to enquire amongst freinds who may bee free to putt their children to him ... .
> [By 1674] It being proposed to this meeting to spare the voyd roome over our meeting house to Lawrance Steele for a schoole roome: this meeting doth with one accord give their concent that he shall have it to the use proposed[13]

One possible way of ensuring a future supply of school-teachers was to 'apprentice' boys to existing Quaker school-masters, so that thereby learning this 'trade', they might themselves eventually run schools in the care of Meetings. The minutes of Meetings show how teachers might be salaried from school fees or out of a combination of fees paid by Meetings, with bequests frequently ear-marked for such purposes.[14]

### (5) Registration of births, marriage and deaths

The compilation of data on individual membership of the Society of Friends through the certification of birth, marriage, death (and transfer of membership) occupies a vast amount of Quaker documentary space, the primary foci for this material being the Monthly Meeting and its records. Their persistence in conducting their own marriages, initially as simple witnessed contracts between spouses, secured for Friends, from as early as 1661, effective control over the ordering and recording of these events, which were otherwise in England normally controlled and enrolled by the established Church. The legitimation of Friends' sectarian marriages secured the legitimacy of children born to those marriages. Friends rejected the need for a visible sacramental baptism and thus they kept no baptismal registers but recorded births. Partly because of the refusals of some parish incumbents to bury Quakers, alleged by some not to be Christians, in hallowed ground, from the earliest period, Friends acquired burial grounds and recorded deaths. Thus, from an early date, opportunities arose for the Society of Friends to operate as a separate community, as far as registration and record were concerned. However, there was still an ultimate responsibility to the law or the state and, if for no other reason, especially with the recording of marriages, there was a real onus on the Quakers to take the tasks of record with the utmost seriousness.

An order of George Fox to keep registers comes from as early as 1656, and some Particular Meeting registers actually do start from around that date, at least having retrospective entries for the births of converts to Quakerism. From about 1668, Monthly Meetings started more systematically to keep registers:

That every Monthly Meeting Buy a Large Convenient Boke for Registring Births Marriages & Burialls, which have been amongst friends since they were a people. And that two faithfull friends of every perticular Meeting may be appointed to see it done by the Monthly Meeting...

In 1669, the Yearly Meeting ordered such books to be kept. Instructions to compile and keep registers continued insistently: in 1675, for instance, the Lancashire Quarterly Meeting required every Monthly Meeting in the county to keep, and to bring to Quarterly Meeting there to be recorded, a register of all births, marriages and deaths. Great exactness was insisted upon in all these proceedings.

New legislation confronted Friends with new requirements. Hardwicke's Marriage Act, coming into effect in 1754 (and remaining in force until 1837) gave statutory validity to Quaker (and Jewish) marriages and their registration. In 1776, the Quakers themselves, through Yearly Meeting, set out a new and more exact method of recording births and deaths: entries from the Particular Meetings were to be filled in on forms, handed into the Monthly Meetings, there entered into registers and then sent on to the Quarterly Meetings, so that Quarterly and Monthly Meetings would have parallel registers, while some Particular Meetings also kept their own registers. The result is, as Peskett says, 'Quaker registers are outstanding, far superior to any other Nonconformist Church'.[15] The sequel, lying outside the period of this survey, is that between 1837 and 1858 the state attempted to gather in all registers, offering in return authentication and legal validity for 'certified copies'. The originals, as we saw in our introduction, were surrendered to the Registrar General and are now lodged in the Public Record Office.

Marriage, as we might expect, occupies one of the fullest areas of Quaker administration and record in the field of registration. The hallmarks of Quaker marriage regulation were permission and consent, for example, the permission of masters for servants to marry, full consultation with Friends on the part of those proposing re-marriage and consent of parents and other relatives as appropriate. The basic documented procedure was for a man to 'publish' his intention of marriage and his intended's consent in his Men's and Women's Particular Meetings, for parental consent to be recorded, for the rights of children from any earlier marriage to be safeguarded, for any prior engagement to be examined, for the financial situation to be established and then for the separate Men's and Women's Monthly Meetings to give approval for the marriage to go ahead - or not. Finally, those present as witnesses signed a certificate that the marriage had taken place.

Clearly, the Quaker documentation on births and deaths was not anything like as full as that on marriages, though apart from recording deaths, the Quakers gave much written attention to regulating the proper, plain conduct of funerals and the arrangements for graveyards and also developed minor literary genres in the forms of testimonies to deceased Friends who had encapsulated the Quaker ideal, and collections of edifying last words. One extension of Quaker registration activities was into the field of probate, with some Monthly Meetings recording wills in which Friends were appointed executors.

One further field of Quaker certification for its members was that of the monitoring of their movements through what were known as 'removal certificates'. Variants of these were used by other denominations, especially the Methodists who from 1765 began issuing a 'Note of Removal' to members migrating from one circuit to another. However, it is doubtful if any other group used the system with the same degree of thoroughness as the Quakers. A removal certificate was a passport sent with a Quaker migrating from one Monthly Meeting to the compass of another (with a receipt from the latter Meeting) establishing the individual's Quaker credentials and requesting the recipient Monthly Meeting's oversight over him or her. In their vast profusion, they provide an unique source for tracing the geographical mobility of considerable numbers of English people, especially in the period of rapid industrialisation and urbanisation towards the end of our period.

Monthly Meetings were the centrepieces in the whole Quaker administrative structure, with their characteristic men's and women's parallel sessions. Many of their functions and records were indeed duplicated by county-level bodies above them and local bodies below them, since duplication and, some would say, over-elaboration were distinguishing marks of Quaker administration.

**Particular Meetings**
The individual local Meeting was the unit in which Friends gathered for their regular worship. They convened, normally once a month, in administrative sessions as Preparative Meetings, preparatory, that is to say, for the Monthly Meeting, to which each Particular Meeting appointed representatives. The recording of Preparative Meeting business in minute books comes later in time than that of Monthly and Quarterly Meetings, generally not until the late 17th or the 18th century. To provide examples, the Leeds series covering our period runs: (1) 1692-1711, (2) 1712-1749, (3) 1749-1792, (4) 1793-1822, (5) 1822-1836, while the Bradford series runs (1) 1698-1715, (2) 1709, (3) 1715-1757, (4) 1758-1797, (5) 1796-1805, (6) 1805-1815, (7) 1816-1823, (8) 1823-1829, (9) 1829-1836.

Women convened their own separate and minuted Preparative Meetings, often in a chamber of a Meeting House or a partitioned loft. For example, the Lancaster series of Women's Particular Meeting Minute Book for our period runs: (1) 1737-1799 (with transcribed letters of George Fox), (2) 1799-1838, and so on, to 1897.

Naturally, the amount of recorded business coming before a Preparative Meeting was normally less than that handled by the bodies higher up the Quaker administrative pyramid. Often the first item on the agenda of Preparative Meeting business was the appointment of representatives to the Monthly Meeting of which it was part. The substantive business was very much that of the other administrative bodies and included: (1) discipline; (2) property and finance; (3) registration and marriages; (4) charity; (5) sufferings and tithes.

## (1)Discipline

The Preparative Meeting was a kind of court of first instance for disciplinary cases which, as we saw earlier, fell mostly in the areas of drink, debt, marital and sexual offences and breaches in the Quaker code of personal simplicity ('plainness'). A disciplinary case begins in the Particular Meeting with a report:

> Willm Cowell & Richard Armistead reported to this Meetting that upon hearing of severall miscariages of Jonathan Merye (viz) of his being overcome with strong drinke & other miscariages, they did speake to him

If necessary, a disciplinary case would be taken by the representatives to the next Monthly Meeting where the disciplinary process would run its course, with the final sanction of expulsion, and the return of a certificate to that effect to the Preparative Meeting where the case had originated.

## (2) Property and finance

The most important piece of a Meeting's property was its Meeting House and parcel of land adjoining, often including a burial ground. Quakers (along with some other Dissenters but to a greater extent) anticipated the 1689 Toleration Act by building Meeting Houses in the 1670s, if not earlier: the penal laws probably even encouraged this development through the heavy fines imposed by the second Conventicle Act, 1670, on the owners of private houses where conventicles were held. Meeting House accounts contain regular items for construction, building alterations and repairs. Like the Monthly Meeting, the Particular Meetings acquired a steady stream of bequests from deceased Friends, funds sometimes being earmarked for such purposes as schooling. Collections were often made for charity and other purposes, for Monthly Meeting expenses and, less frequently, for Quarterly Meeting or national 'stock'. There was an annual audit, and deficits arising from the Meeting treasurer's authorised expenditure would be made good by collections.

## (3) Registration and marriage

As we saw, Preparative Meetings might keep their own transcripts of local births, marriages and deaths, copies of the entries that were sent on to the superior meeting, after verbal announcement of the event at the Preparative Meeting. A Particular Meeting possessing a burial ground might keep a register like the one at Colthouse in North Lancashire, and other documentary responsibilities would arise, such as compliance with the 1679 Act of Parliament for Burial in Woollens.

A Preparative Meeting played a vital role in marriage as the place where the carefully graduated process leading to a wedding started with the man's announcing his plans in the separate women's and then the men's Preparative Meetings. As the local body that knew the parties in question most intimately, the Particular Meeting was a useful agency for screening would-be spouses in a process somewhat resembling that of calling bans of marriage:

> Joshua Arthington having lade before this Meeting his intention of marrage with Deborah Moore (a Member of York Monthly Meeting) & it appearing by note from her that it was with her concent, having also concent of

relations is left to his libourty to lye the same before the Monthly Meeting ...

## (4) Charity

Although the Monthly Meeting was the primary unit for the actual administration of Friends' charity, the Preparative Meeting was often in a better position to know the details of particular cases of need, and to discern 'deserving' from less deserving applicants:

> ...whether it were convenient to allow Bridget Taylor a maintenance or not except he [sic] would endeavour more then shee does to get her livelihood, and some friends intimating that they fear it was more sloth then exercise of mind that was the cause of her indisposition,...

Charity transactions included responses to charitable 'briefs', official documents which, though sometimes fraudulently abused, set a seal of state approval on appeals for assistance for disaster victims, refugees from persecution abroad and the like. Within the Preparative Meetings too, collections were taken for named individual Friends who had suffered by floods, fires or other accidents, either within the Meeting in question or farther afield. Apprenticeships considered as charity cases tended to be handled by the Monthly and Quarterly Meetings which acted more efficiently as clearing houses in that kind of administrative work.

## (5) Sufferings and tithes

The Preparative Meeting was the obvious place for the primary collection of information about Friends' position vis-à-vis tithes and other church charges. The material falls into two closely related categories: (i) financial and factual digests of privations (imprisonments, assaults, etc.) and of goods lost by distraint as a result of Friends' refusal to pay such charges; and (ii) statements of refusal to pay and the grounds for such refusal. Annual assemblies of heads of households were held within the Particular Meetings to set both categories of information on record, in advance of Monthly Meeting.

Our survey of the records of the various strata of Quaker Meetings has concentrated, as has been the case throughout this survey of Nonconformist archives, on formal reports of business meetings in the form of special minute books. For reasons of space, much has had to be omitted from our study of the Quaker material. There are, for example, other minute book series, such as those of proliferating bodies like the Ministers and Elders (lay leaders of worship and church officers) whose sessions at Monthly and Quarterly level were faithfully recorded. Then too, great collections are extant of loose-leaf material and correspondence covering finance, building maintenance, charitable expenditure, reports from Quaker schools, support papers in disciplinary cases, documentation on the Friends' unfolding involvement in enlightened social concerns such as anti-slavery, and the majestic series of Yearly Meeting minutes, 'advices' and epistles on every aspect of the lives of Quakers. With its largely silent Meetings for Worship, the Society of Friends has left us the most vocal records of the whole of English Nonconformity in our period.

## Notes to Chapter VI

1. See Craig Horle, 'Judicial Encounters with Quakers, 1660-1688', *Journal of the Friends Historical Society*, liv (1976-82), pp. 85-100.

2. F.G. Emmison, *Guide to the Essex Record Office* (Chelmsford, 1969), p. 117; William le Hardy, ed., *Hertfordshire County Records. Calendar to the Sessions Books, Sessions Minute Books and other Records*, vol. vi, 1658-1700 (Hertford, 1930), p. 384.

3. Helen Forde, 'Friends and Authority: A consideration of attitudes and expedients with particular reference to Derbyshire', *Journal of the Friends Historical Society*, liv (1976-82), pp. 115-125.

4. Melanie Barber, 'Records of Quaker Interest in Lambeth Palace Library', *Journal of the Friends Historical Society*, liii (1972-75), pp. 166-7.

5. Watts, *The Dissenters*, pp. 269-270.

6. Quaker records themselves sometimes, albeit unconsciously, provide some of the aptest commentary on this profusion of Quaker Meetings. Typical is a minute from the Lancaster Monthly Meeting, for 1701: 'Something here being discoursed concerning a general meeting for the 4 meetings at this monthly meetings it's referred to our next monthly meeting.'

7. Russell S. Mortimer, *Alphabetical Index and Copy of the Catalogue of the Contents of the Safe at the Friends Meeting House, Charlton Hill, Leeds....* (Leeds, 1972); Michael Mullett and Ralph Randles, *Inventory of Documents... Kept in the Friends Meeting House, Lancaster* (Lancaster, 1976).

8. See [Anon.], 'Settlement of London Yearly Meeting', *Journal of the Friends Historical Society*, ii (1905), pp. 59-63.

9. Richard E. Stagg, 'Friends' Queries and General Advices. A Survey of their Development in London Yearly Meeting, 1682-1860', *Journal of the Friends Historical Society*, xlix (1959-61), pp. 209-235. For a glossary of Quaker terms such as 'Truth', 'First Publishers of Truth', 'convincement' etc., see *The First Minute Book of the Gainsborough Monthly Meeting of the Society of Friends, 1669-1719*, ed. Harold Brace, Lincolnshire Record Soc. xxxviii-xl (1939), i, pp. xxii-xxiii.

10. Each Monthly Meeting sent at least two, with a customary maximum of six, representatives, to Quarterly Meeting. In 1716, Yorkshire's 14 Monthly Meetings sent a total of 39 representatives to a county Quarterly Meeting.

11.    Nicholas Morgan, 'The Social and Political Relations of the Lancaster
       Quaker Community, 1688-1740', in Michael Mullett, ed., *Early Lancaster
       Friends* (Lancaster, 1978), p. 28; W. Pearson Thistlethwaite, *Yorkshire
       Quarterly Meeting (of the Society of Friends) 1665-1966* (Harrogate,
       1979), p. 24.

12.    *Minute Book of the Men's Meeting of the Society of Friends in Bristol,
       1667-1686*, ed. Russell Mortimer, Bristol Record Soc., xxvi (1971), pp.
       xx, 4, 5, 25, 31, 105. See also Ruth Dove and Helen Segebarth, *A History
       of the Friends' Meeting House, Lancaster*, (Lancaster 1991) and David
       Butler, *Quaker Meeting Houses of the Lake Counties*, (London,1978).

13.    *Ibid.*, pp. 57, 85.

14.    Ralph Randles, '"Faithful Friends and well qualified". The Early Years
       of the Friends' School at Lancaster', in Mullett, ed., *Early Lancaster
       Friends*, pp. 33-42.

15.    Peskett, *Guide to the Parish and Non-Parochial Registers*, pp. xli, xliii.

**Sources for Chapter VI**

References in this chapter include the following printed, manuscript and
typescript sources:

F.H.L. *(transcript)* Morning Meeting Minutes 1692-1700 and Six Weeks' Meeting
Minutes, vols.1-19 (1671-1836); typescript index.

L.R.O.: Selection of Advices from Yearly Meeting, Lancaster Monthly Meeting
Minute Books, 1675-1718, Lancashire Quarterly Meeting Minute Books, 1669-1711;
*The First Minute Book of the Gainsborough Monthly Meeting of the Society of
Friends', 1669-1719*, ed. Harold Brace, Lincolnshire Record Soc., xxxviii-xl (1939);
(typescript) W. Pearson Thistlethwaite, Yorkshire Quarterly Meeting (of the Society
of Friends) 1665-1966 (Harrogate, 1979).

F.H.L.: London and Middlesex Quarterly Meeting.

L.R.O.: A Book for the Women's Quarterly Meeting in Lancashire, 1675-1777;
Lancashire Friends' Financial Papers, 1692-1804; *Leeds Friends Minute Book 1692
to 1712*, eds. Jean and Russell Mortimer, Yorks. Archaeological Soc., Record Ser.,
cxxxix (1977-8); Lancaster Particular Meeting Minute Book, 1698-1740; Dilworth
Abbatt, *Quaker Annals of Preston and the Fylde* (London, 1931); Elizabeth J.
Satterthwaite, *Records of the Friends' Burial Ground at Colthouse* (Ambleside,
1914).

F.H.L.: Craig W. Horle, A Listing of the Original Records of Sufferings, 1976.

Important editions of Meeting minutes in print are: *The Somerset Quarterly*

Important editions of Meeting minutes in print are: *The Somerset Quarterly Meeting of the Society of Friends 1668-1699*, ed. Stephen C. Morland, Somerset Record Soc., lxxv (1978); *Minute Book of the Men's Meeting of the Society of Friends in Bristol, 1686-1704*, ed. Russell Mortimer, Bristol Record Soc., xxx (1977); *Minute Book of the Monthly Meeting of the Society of Friends for the Upperside of Buckinghamshire, 1669-1690*, ed. B.S.Snell, Buckinghamshire Archaeological Soc., i, 1937. Note also the important Calendar and Index by Geoffrey Nuttall, D.D., of the Swarthmore MSS. at the Library of the Society of Friends in London, typescript, 1952. The Society's journal is the *Journal of the Friends Historical Society*, 1903. See also Edward Milligan, 'Society of Friends Records', *Archives*, v, 1961, pp. 11-12.

Quaker material is available in considerable profusion in various record offices. To take a few examples, the Lancashire Record Office holds the Quaker archive from Lancaster which contains a wealth of material on Lancaster Particular Meeting, the county's Monthly Meetings and its Quarterly Meeting. Kent County Archives have Kent Quarterly Meeting minutes, 1733-1943, Kent Women's Quarterly Meeting minutes, 1795-1850, trust property registers, c. 1767-1836, minutes from the county's four Monthly Meetings and material from three Particular Meetings. Essex Record Office holds (in microfilm) Essex Quarterly Meeting Minutes, 1694-1854, and accounts and other material (minutes etc.) from Witham, Coggeshall, Colchester, Felsted and Thaxted Monthly Meetings. Friends' House London had important epistolary material on individual Friends, for example: the clerk of London Yearly Meeting, George Stacey (1786-1857), and correspondence pertaining to the leading Quaker women Martha Routh (1743-1817) and Elizabeth Robson (1771-1843). Note also the correspondence (including family letters) of Henry Tuke (1755-1815) in the Borthwick Institute, York.

**CHAPTER VII**

## THE RECORDS OF THE SMALLER UNESTABLISHED CHURCHES

### Introduction

So far in this survey we have dealt with the records of major Protestant denominations outside the Church of England. In this conclusion, we shall briefly consider some types of archival material engendered by numerically smaller bodies.

The smaller Nonconformist churches tend to fall into three categories. In the first group are those religious communities which came into existence during the English religious revolution of the 1640s and 1650s and which survived for a shorter or longer period thereafter. Some groupings in this category, such as the Fifth Monarchists, were essentially the products of a unique time, while in the case of another group, the Ranters, it has been argued that they were a figment of hostile propaganda and did not really exist at all.[1] Our second category consists of Protestant religious bodies brought to England through foreign immigration, usually by victims of persecution in France, the southern Netherlands, the German lands and Central Europe. Our third category consists of movements emerging as a result of England's second major religious awakening, the Evangelical movement of the eighteenth century.

It should be said that we are dealing with religious groups organised enough to leave a written record, rather than with the less traceable persistence of underlying attitudes which often fed newly emergent bodies with recruits, in the way a Lollard tradition may have fed into the General Baptists or the earlier Seeker movement may have engendered Quakerism. The enormous importance of the 1640s and 1650s should also be taken into account, since not only did new creations like the Quakers evolve in that period, but pre-existent phenomena, such as the Baptist churches, owe much of their growth and rise to those two decades. As for that novel movement, the Society of Friends, it can be regarded as in some ways a kind of vehicle for the perpetuation of the multifarious religious (and socio-political) radicalism of the revolutionary decades.

### The Muggletonians

Ephemerality seems to be almost a necessary hazard confronting many separatist churches. After all, even the great Presbyterian church, with over six hundred congregations in the early eighteenth century, was threatened with a kind of group extinction in the face of a theological revisionism that submerged its pristine doctrinal principles. It is all the more remarkable then, that a religious community - the Muggletonians - formed in 1652 and with perhaps three hundred members at the end of the seventeenth century, should have survived until the death of the 'last Muggletonian' in 1979, leaving a vast archival record.

Fascinating as the durability of the Muggletonians over three centuries is, the survival and re-discovery in the 1970s of their archives in 88 or 89 volumes, forms a veritable romance, told too well by Professor Lamont to be repeated here.[2]

Purchased and now housed in the British Library,[3] the Muggletonian archive can be sub-divided for purposes of analysis into four parts. The early material includes letters of the founders of the sect, John Reeve (1608-1698) and Lodowick Muggleton (1609-1698). These letters, which were highly authoritiative in guiding the life of this religious community, were repeatedly transcribed in the 17th, 18th and 19th centuries. In addition, the Muggletonian archive contains treatises by the two founders and other influential figures in the movement. The Muggletonians placed great emphasis on worship by means of 'spiritual songs', and the archive contains a lavish collection of these congregational hymns. More prosaically, the fourth part of the Muggletonian archive consists of administrative material for, as Professor Lamont says, 'the Muggletonians were great hoarders. They preserved every piece of information they could...'[4]. Thus the section of the archive designated 'Accounts' consists of lists of gifts and legacies, quarterly subscriptions, internal poor relief payments, expenses on premises, printing bills, library lists, and, since the Muggletonians were notably convivial, lists and bills for their festivals and the annual dinners for which they were mildly famous. Much of their administrative material comes from the 19th century, but the whole archive, as Lamont says, provides 'a consecutive set of pieces of evidence as to the life of the sect from about 1700 to 1900', including, for example, information about a secession in the 1770s. The re-emergence of the Muggletonian archive is one of the most remarkable archival discoveries in recent years. The British Library's acquisition also includes some works of the prophets Reeve and Muggleton printed between 1652 and 1822.

### Immigrant churches

Throughout its history, English Protestantism has been constantly nourished by refugee immigration from the continent. Two linked francophone groups were the Walloons, originating in the Low Countries, and the French Huguenots, numbers of whom migrated to England as a result of Louis XIV's revocation in 1685 of the toleration charter of the French Protestants, the 1598 Edict of Nantes. Many of these French-speaking Protestants from the Calvinist tradition found neither the liturgy nor the episcopalianism of the Church of England as objectionable as did many English Calvinists, so that some Huguenot and Walloon communities were conformists and used the Book of Common Prayer, perhaps in its officially approved French translation. However, in the West Country, for example, there were Nonconformist Huguenot congregations, similar to Independency or Presbyterianism, and producing some records. In Dartmouth such a community grew up after 1689, numbering about 130 in 1715 and eventually merging with the local Presbyterians, so that its existence was partly recorded in the Presbyterian registers, starting in 1726 and now in the P.R.O. Some material on its ministry is in the Exeter Diocesan Archives, now in Devon Record Office, Exeter. In Exeter itself, a Nonconformist Huguenot congregation was established in 1682, numbered around 120 in 1716, and thereafter joined the Exeter United Brethren, some of its registration entries being found in that body's register and others in the register of St Olave's church, Exeter. In Plymouth, a large community numbering 500 in 1715 emerged after 1681, surviving until 1672; it had no registers of its own but its births were recorded in those of neighbouring parish churches.[5]

On the South Coast, the chapel known in Southampton as 'God's House' was given to refugees from persecution in the Netherlands in 1567. The community expanded as result of subsequent immigration from the Channel Islands and France. Structurally and culturally, if not doctrinally, Nonconformist until 1712, this 'French Church' kept a register from 1567, including lists of communicants and also historical reflections. The series of baptisms runs from 1567 to 1779 and the burials from 1567 to 1722; the lengthy series of marriages, from 1567 to 1753, is all the more valuable in that the places of origin in France of marriage partners are given.[6] The pattern we have looked at in the West Country Huguenot/Walloon churches suggests that the Southampton 'French Church' was exceptional in the exhaustiveness of its registration documentation.

### The Moravians

This small immigrant church of pre-Reformation central European origin was established as a minority community in England from 1728 and moved towards a Nonconformist position from the 1740s. One example of its existence and record is the congregation at James St., Devonport, established in 1768 and incorporating an earlier Plymouth community. Its baptism and birth registers for 1785-1836 are in the P.R.O., and other records entered from ministers' diaries are at Moravian Church House, London. Also at Moravian Church House is the correspondence of the English Moravian founder James Hutton (1715-1795) with Benjamin Ingham, the Wesleyans and others (about 33 bundles). See also the letters, concerning missions in America, addressed to the Moravian Christopher Ignatius Latrobe (1758-1836), at Moravian Church House, and his journal (1788-9 and 1792) at John Rylands Library, Manchester.

### The Inghamites

A number of smaller, indigenous religious bodies came into existence during the great upsurge in Evangelical revivalism in the 18th century. It is a measure of the importance of personal charisma in these groups that they sometimes took their names from their leaders and founders. The Inghamites, for example, derived their title from their founder, Benjamin Ingham (1712-1772). Ingham was a Oxford Methodist pioneer in the 1730s and initially close to the Wesleys. However, his spirituality was close to that of the Moravians. Ingham, who evangelised sucessfully in the North, merged his fellowship with the Moravians in 1742 but subsequently took some 80 of these congregations out of the Moravian connection and into an independent 'Inghamite' church, with its local societies under the loose presidency of the leader. A further split brought many groups into Methodism, so that well before the end of the 18th century the Inghamite movement was in some decay.

Nevertheless, communities survived, perhaps a little indomitably, into the 19th century. One such was the Inghamite church in Kendal's Pear Tree Meeting House, a community with an impressive and absorbing archival record. It was a community that clearly had a strong sense of its own sectarian identity and of its past, recording its origins (probably in 1756), its purchase of a barn as a meeting place, and its first baptism, by Benjamin Ingham himself. An early elder, it was recalled, 'left the connexion having espoused the mode of speaking of the Godhead adapted by James Allen who had previously seceded from Messrs. Ingham and Batty on the same subject...'.[7]

Thus the archive of a small, even marginal, Northern gathered church may contain a wealth of unsuspected material, including insights into the doctrinal squabbles of members and elders. If the social identity of the (part-time) ministers and elders is anything to go by, the church had an overwhelmingly plebeian membership: one 'gentleman of some property' but, more typically, a shoemaker, a yeoman farmer or two, a tanner. A somewhat isolated sect, the Inghamites were all too aware of the disapproval of some of their peculiarities, as at an internment in 1756 when a 'Miscellaneous and not approving concourse of people [expressed] astonishment that a Woman should be buried in the Corner of a field...'.

Such recollections, entered as memoranda enclosed within the church's account book, convey a sharp clarity of atmosphere and incident, as does the following evocative description, from the same source:

> Ordination  On Friday the 29th day of October, in the Year of our Lord one thousand eight hundred and thirty Robert Dent and Thomas Levens, were set apart to the Elder's Office, over the Inghamite Church assem bling in the Pear Tree Chapel, Kendal.
>
> The Church met at 8 °clock in the morning fasting and commenced worship by singing the 74th Hymn... Henry Clegg, one of the Elders from Wheatley Lane, engaged in prayer.
> Joseph Nicholson, Elder of the Church in Leeds, read appropriate portions of Scripture for the occasion; and then proceeded to offer an Ordination prayer which was accompanied by the Imposition of the hands of the Elders on the Heads of the new pastors kneeling. John Huck, the resident Elder was present but owing to Age and Infirmities did not take any part, in the laying on of hands... The service was closed with singing and prayer, and had deeply interested all who were present, as was visibly manifest by the close attention to the aforesaid scriptural addresses, during their delivery.

## Notes to Chapter VII

1.      J.C. Davis, *Fear, Myth and History, The Ranters and the Historians* (Cambridge, 1986).

2.      William Lamont, 'The Muggletonian Archive', in Christopher Hill, William Lamont and Barry Reay, *The World of the Muggletonians* (London, 1983), pp. 1-5.

3.      Add. MSS. 60207-60230. See also the List and Index Society Special Series, vol. xv, 1982: 'Rough Register' of acquisitions by the Department of Manuscripts, British Library, 1976-1980.

4.      Lamont, 'The Muggletonian Archive', p. 3.

5.      Peskett, *Guide to Parish and Non-Parochial Registers....*, pp. lxv ff., 230.

6.      For the register of this church, see *Régistre de l' église Wallonne de Southampton*, ed. H.M. Godfray, Huguenot Soc. of London Quarto Ser., iv (1890); for its minutes, especially during its last Nonconformist phase, *The Minute Book of the French Church at Southampton 1702-1939*, ed. E. Welch, *Southampton Record* Ser., xxvi (1983).

7.      C.R.R.: Kendal Inghamites: *Account Book of Receipts... 1855-1877* (inside cover: *Sketches and Memorandums*.) For Benjamin Ingham, see R.W. Thompson, *Benjamin Ingham* (Kendal, 1958), and D.F. Clarke, 'Benjamin Ingham, 1712-72', *Proceedings of the Wesley Hist. Soc.*, xxxvii (1972).